SUPER JUICE

Beverley Piper is a freelance home economist who started writing about microwave cookery when working as a microwave oven demonstrator; she also presented a BBC series on microwave cookery. She develops and writes recipes and presents food for display and photography. She is the author of *Fast and Easy Food for Busy People*, due to be published in June 1993, and *Beverley Piper's Quick and Easy Healthy Cookery*, published in 1992. Beverley Piper lives in Kent.

Also by Beverley Piper

Fast and Easy Food for Busy People
Beverley Piper's Quick and Easy Healthy Cookery

Super Juice

Juicing Recipes for Health and Vitality

Beverley Piper

HEADLINE

First published in 1993
by HEADLINE BOOK PUBLISHING PLC

10 9 8 7 6 5 4 3 2

ISBN 0 7472 4098 1

Typeset by Keyboard Services, Luton

Printed and bound in Great Britain by
HarperCollins Manufacturing, Glasgow

HEADLINE BOOK PUBLISHING PLC
Headline House
79 Great Titchfield Street
London W1P 7FN

Contents

Super Juice

Introduction

Every home should have one – there is simply no doubt about it! My centrifugal juicing machine now sits permanently on the work surface, close to both the sink and the rubbish bin, and has become an exciting and very welcome part of our everyday lives.

Simplicity itself to use and easy to empty and clean, the juicer swallows speedily prepared fruits and vegetables and turns them into the most delicious and healthy juices you have ever tasted. Juicing machines are so clever and the health benefits offered so great, that I'm quite sure you will soon be just as ardent a fan of juicing as I am.

These juicers, which all have attractive design lines, remind me visually of the food processor. They vary slightly from manufacturer to manufacturer, so it pays to have a good look at all the machines available before you buy. Some, for instance, offer a filling tray which doubles as a cover when the juicer is not in use and, as this tray acts as a store for the prepared fruit and vegetables prior to juicing, owners of such machines will not need a mixing bowl as a store (see recipes). Certain manufacturers offer a foam separator or baffle to remove the foam (some are detachable, so you can choose whether to use it or not); at home we all enjoy drinking the foam.

Buying a new gadget is always a bit of a gamble; no one wants to buy something that will prove to be a one-minute wonder, that the family will use once or twice and then gradually push further and further towards the back of the cupboard until it ends up on a table at the local boot sale. Take my word for it, that is not what will happen to your juicer. However, you will also find a section of recipes in the book that use the food processor. You might like to try out one or two of these before investing in a juicer. I have selected recipes that have proved very popular with my family and friends, and that show the versatility of the blender.

I hope to be able to show you just some of the advantages of juicing machines and of the healthy and delicious juices they produce. The juicer is easy to use and efficient and the resulting juices are delicious and versatile; different members of the family can prepare their own favourite healthy juice combinations without having to empty the machine of debris (until it's full of course). I believe this machine will shortly find a home in many British households where it will be used to the full.

In the mid-1960s, when I was about twelve years old, I can remember my mother returning from a holiday spent at a nature cure centre in Scotland. She was full of the virtues of brown bread and carrot juice and sadly I labelled her a bit of a crank, as I couldn't imagine what carrot juice would look like, let alone how it would taste.

Of course, we had no way of producing juice at home, so my mother slowly forgot about her carrot juice. I do so wish that she was still around now so that I could provide her with as much of this healthy and delicious juice as she could ever possibly want and tell her that I totally agree with her.

BUYING YOUR JUICER

Continuous juice extractors are available in the UK from Kenwood, Braun, Phillips and Moulinex. They retail at between £39 and £45 approximately. Before buying, check that the machine will suit your needs; consider capacity and actual size as well as how easy the machine will be to dismantle and clean.

Kenwood

This company offers juicers in two sizes: the JE 500 is the smaller model with a 700ml (1¼ pints) capacity, whilst the JE 600 has a capacity of 2.5kg (5lb). Both Kenwood models offer a choice of two motor speeds, one for hard textures such as apples, carrots etc., and one for soft fruits such as pineapples, strawberries and kiwi fruits. There is a safety locking device and a collecting jug with an anti-froth baffle to strain the juice as you pour, providing an instantly cleaner juice which some may prefer.

Braun

The Braun MP 80 offers a feeder tray, especially useful for large quantities of produce, and is capable of processing up to 4kg (9lb) apples at one time. This feeder tray doubles as a useful dust cover. The collection beaker has a capacity of 500ml (17fl oz) and has a built-in foam separator for those who prefer cleaner juice. Also provided are a plunger, safety lock and cord storage.

One speed is offered on the Braun machine, which is suitable for most types of fruits and vegetables, but Braun advise against juicing red- and blackcurrants and rhubarb and suggest that special steam presses are better suited to types of fruit that have a particularly high pectin content.

Moulinex
Moulinex offer continuous juice extractors in two sizes. The 753 top-of-the-range model has a large 1.3 litre (2¼ pints) capacity with flex storage. The 864 model is smaller with a 700ml (1¼ pints) capacity and a useful integral jug, with a handle, that collects the juice. There is a plunger and a safety lock on both models. The smaller model is particularly useful for those with limited worktop space as it is unobtrusive, yet powerful. Moulinex do not offer the baffle facility that takes away the foam, but I stir it into the juice and find it delicious and creamy. The Moulinex is particularly quick and easy to clean and re-assemble.

Phillips
The HR 2820 juice extractor has special safety locks and provides a choice so you can choose whether you want your juice with or without a foam top. It will cope with large quantities before it needs to be emptied and provides you with a special brush for easy cleaning of the filter unit. The Phillips juicer is attractive and has integrated and easy to empty juice and pulp containers.

How do they work?
Varying slightly in component parts, the juicing machines all work by the same principles. With the motor running, the fruits and vegetables to be juiced are fed through a feed tube by means of a plastic plunger. The juicer extracts all the liquid with its vitamins and minerals out of the produce by centrifugal force, in the same way that a spin-dryer spins water out of clothes. This juice is instantly filtered and passed through into a receptacle, usually a jug provided, ready to be drunk straight away. The residue of the fruit and vegetables is deposited in the hopper or pulp store, which again varies from machine to machine; some are on the top, others are situated towards the side of the juicer. Emptying the hopper is simple, although on some machines you have to release the safety arms and lift off the top of the

machine, which forms the hopper. In others, the receptacle is to the side of the unit and it should simply be emptied when it looks full. I use a plastic spatula to scrape the residue, which ends up pretty dry, into the bin.

Cleaning is quick and easy. Simply unlock the safety arms and take the removable components to the sink to be washed with washing up liquid, using a brush to clean the re-usable filter. The plastic parts may become discoloured when processing food with a high pigment content, such as carrots, but this can be cleaned off using vegetable oil and kitchen roll.

The motor housing unit should never be immersed in water. To clean, take the plug out of the socket first, then wipe the unit with a damp cloth.

Compact citrus juicers

These are available from Braun, Krups, Phillips, Moulinex and Kenwood and are very much like a sophisticated version of the glass or plastic hand juicers we have had in the kitchen for years. A plastic cone fits over a perspex jug which locks on to an electrical unit. As you switch on the machine and press half a citrus fruit on to the cone, it rotates and the juice will be extracted and pass through the strainer into the jug below. When the fruit is removed from the cone, the motor turns off automatically.

On the Braun Citromatic Compact, which has a jug with a capacity of 350ml (12fl oz), there is also a simple way of adjusting the amount of fruit pulp in the juice. Large models, with a capacity of 600ml (1 pint), are also available.

Serving the juice is simple: remove the jug from the machine by swivelling the handle, lift off the cone and strainer and pour the juice into glasses. One large orange yields approximately 150ml (5fl oz) orange juice which seems plenty for one person at breakfast time.

Always disconnect the machine from the mains before cleaning, for safety's sake. Then disassemble the machine, cleaning the motor block with a damp cloth and washing up all the remaining parts.

Families who drink a lot of orange juice will definitely love the citrus juicers. Retailing at approximately £14.99, they are quick to assemble and operate and take up very little space. The jugs are easy to pour from and the resulting juice is full of vitamin C and is completely natural.

Positioning of the juicer/equipment needed
The juicer should be placed on a worktop that is near the sink and a disposal bin. Obviously, as it runs on electricity, it needs a nearby socket to plug into.

Allow room around the machine for a chopping board – white polyethylene ones are best as they are far easier to clean and more hygienic than wooden boards. You'll need space for a large mixing bowl too, for the prepared fruit or vegetables. It's important to have the rubbish bin nearby as you will have to empty the hopper several times if you are making juice for a number of people. You may, of course, prefer to put the fruit and vegetable waste on to a compost heap. A sharp knife and some attractive glasses are the only other things necessary for the would-be juicer and, of course, a supply of ice in the freezer.

THE BENEFITS OF JUICING
When asked about fruit juice, most of us think of the products we purchase in cartons and bottles from supermarkets. By law, these commercial juices are pasteurised to kill off enzymes and extend the juices' shelf lives, making them a marketable proposition. Heat destroys fragile vitamin C, so synthetic vitamin C is added by manufacturers, often alongside water and sugar, after pasteurisation.

Drinks to most Britons probably mean coffee and tea and maybe alcohol and water. Coffee and tea are both acid forming and contain stimulants. The quality of tap water is debatable and varies from area to area in its composition. Natural spring and mineral waters bought bottled are a fairly good option.

Fruit and vegetable juices are high in vitamins and minerals; they are also alkaline and excellent refreshers. Many juices aid digestion and assist the system in the absorption of nutrients from foods. Some juices, such as grape juice, aid constipation sufferers.

As fruit juices are delicious at any time of the day (and night for insomniacs) and can be diluted to taste with mineral or tap water if required, there is every incentive to drink them.

Having a glass of red or white wine with a meal relaxes us, aids digestion and has now been linked with helping to thin the blood so that it passes easily around the body. Unfortunately, it is not easy to drink just one glass. Excess alcohol is fattening: a 150ml (5fl oz) glass of wine contains 80–90 Kcals. Alcohol also tends to magnify allergic conditions, it's dehydrating and can result in a thick head in the morning! Perhaps it's better to stick to juice, especially as it's so delicious and just as great a treat as any alcoholic drink.

If this is not enough to convince you to invest in a juicer, just compare the taste of a glass of juice bought from the supermarket with one made on a juicing machine. There is simply no comparison.

To make orange and apple juice
Peel three heavy, ripe oranges, leaving about half the pith still on the orange you are going to juice as it contains both vitamins and minerals. Cut the oranges into slices that will fit the machine. Discard the pips, but leave all the membrane intact. Now wash and slice two Granny Smith apples to fit the juicer, without peeling or coring.

With the motor running juice the oranges and apples, using the plunger. In seconds you will have approximately 300ml (½ pint) of the most delicious tasting, pale golden frothy juice that positively shouts out 'health' and 'zing'. More importantly the juice will be full of goodness: vitamin C, vitamin B complex, potassium, zinc and phosphorus.

Fruit also contains fructose, or natural fruit sugar, so the juice will taste deliciously sweet, yet be refreshing – a shade different from the rather flat tasting product from the shop.

When you begin to use the juicer there are several things that strike you immediately.

Health
You have only to sip your first glass of fruit or vegetable juice to be hit by a feeling of sheer vitality – it may sound corny but it's true. The machine extracts all the food value and taste from the produce and deposits it in the jug ready to be poured into a glass and drunk. The sensation is of biting into a ripe juicy apple. There is no need to stop eating apples as they, and any other raw fruit or vegetables for that matter, are excellent foods full of vitamins, minerals, natural sugars and fibre, which we all need. However, as you drink the juice be aware that the machine has done what the body does slightly more slowly to fruits and vegetables.

8

It has digested them and squeezed out all the goodness that goes directly into your bloodstream *fast*.

Digestion by the human body is a fairly slow process: food is masticated and ptyalin, an enzyme in the saliva, acts on starch in foods commencing the chemical breakdown and converting it into sugar. It's then rolled into a bolus by the tongue and swallowed. The digestive process continues in the stomach where food remains for three to four hours, then in the small and large intestine. Finally the waste product ends up in the bowel.

Drinking juice from a juicer enables carbohydrate, plus the vitamins and minerals, to pass straight into the bloodstream in its liquid state; it's no wonder it gives you a lift quickly.

Don't store juice – precious vitamin C is lost very quickly so, to ensure the maximum benefit from juice, it must be drunk immediately. I find that an ice cube or two makes all the juices more refreshing.

Speed
With ingredients ready washed, juicing is wonderfully speedy. A chopping board, a sharp knife, a mixing bowl and a couple of glasses are all that's needed for almost instant drinks; it's easier than making tea! Also, very few ingredients need peeling; all the goodness in and just below the skins of fruit and vegetables goes into the juice as well.

Another advantage is that there is no flavour transference from one batch of juice to the next (as long as the jug is rinsed between recipes), so three or four different juices can be prepared one after the other.

Variety
The variety of juices is even larger than the many varieties of fruit and vegetables available. Experiment with all sorts of combinations, coming up with an exciting new flavour every time; have fun too, using the juices in a variety of ways.

Juices in cooking
In the book you will find plenty of recipes for cooking that incorporate juices. Because of the ease and speed of preparation and the wonderful taste, juices can be used

daily as bases to sauces, sweet and savoury, especially for stir-fry recipes that need a quick tasty sauce. Ice cream is delicious with a fruit sauce either served directly from the juicer jug as it is, or heated and thickened with a little arrowroot. Hot and cold soups such as the Gazpacho recipe (see p. 119) are deliciously refreshing and many of the vegetable juices will enhance the next casserole or soup you make. Try sorbets made from juices and also fruits lightly stewed in juice. Add a scoop of ice cream to the fruit juices for instant desserts that taste divine.

The superb flavour of juice makes it a very useful ingredient, and it is also extremely versatile. Try the Fruits of the Forest Sorbet (see p. 167) and the Speedy Beef Casserole (see p. 159) which is wonderful served with the Tomato and Olive Oil Bread recipe (see p. 161).

Once you've tried your hand at some of these recipes, enjoy experimenting with your own variations.

VITAMINS

Vitamins help to control the many chemical reactions that continually take place in our bodies. They exist in just about every food we eat, in varying quantities and are, indeed, vital to life itself. Lack of vitamins can lead to disease, e.g. lack of vitamin C, in severe cases, causes scurvy. There are 13 vitamins essential to the human diet and healthy eating will supply our bodies with all of them without the need to take supplements. Fresh juice is an excellent source of essential vitamins and minerals, so enjoy drinking it in the knowledge that it's doing you good.

These are brief notes that are not intended as any kind of medical guide and should not be used as such.

Vitamin A

Is essential, with protein, for healthy growth and replacement of tissue. It is important in the prevention of premature ageing, for healing tissue, to prevent infection, particularly of the nose and throat, and it helps eyesight. Important for healthy liver and kidneys. *Source:* Milk, butter, margarine, fish oils, eggs, liver, kidney, fresh green vegetables, such as broccoli and spinach, tomatoes and melon.

10

Vitamin B complex
Essential for a healthy nervous system, it can help to lift depression. Also vital for skin, hair and clear eyes. Particularly important for women suffering from premenstrual tension.

Vitamin B1
Important for the production of energy and in toning the whole nervous system. *Source:* Milk, eggs, yeast, nuts, beans, most meat, leafy greens and sprouts.

Vitamin B2
Essential for healthy skin and eyes, good for hair. Helps growth. *Source:* Milk, eggs, yeast, green vegetables, cereals, bread, fish.

Vitamin B3
Useful in dispersing arthritis. Essential for a healthy brain, needed by the nervous system. *Source:* Milk, eggs, nuts, cereals, leafy green vegetables.

Vitamin B12
Promotes growth in children, helps body produce new red blood cells. Keeps nerves healthy. *Source:* Milk, liver, meat, eggs, fish, yeast.

Vitamin C
Helps wounds to heal and is essential for all connective tissue found in the body (cartilage, tendons, ligaments, etc.). Has preventive and curing properties against colds; it is also an anti-stress vitamin, and it helps cure stomach upsets. *Source:* Oranges, lemons, strawberries, blackcurrants, potatoes, tomatoes, fresh green vegetables, red and green peppers, cauliflower.

Vitamin D
Essential for absorption of calcium and therefore keeps gums and teeth healthy. Necessary for the thyroid gland. *Source:* Fish oils, margarine, eggs, butter, sunlight on skin.

Vitamin E
Vital to prevent destruction by the body of fat-soluble vitamins. A natural anti-coagulant, helping blood flow freely, therefore preventing thrombosis and heart disease. Essential for reproduction. Good for healthy skin and known to aid menstrual disorders. *Source:* Vegetables, particularly leafy greens, celery and carrots; wholemeal bread, rice, eggs, butter.

Vitamin K
Essential for blood clotting and important for maintaining a healthy liver. *Source:* Liver, dark green vegetables, kelp.

MINERALS
Minerals, found in the soil, are essential for life. Humans take in minerals by eating plants and also by eating animals which have ingested plants and absorbed minerals from them. Juices are an alternative excellent and natural source.

Minerals go straight into our bloodstream via the walls of the intestines and are necessary for general health. There are seven that humans need in fairly large quantities and a further 14 trace minerals that we need in minute quantities. As with vitamins, a normal healthy diet will provide the body with all it needs, but it is interesting to know a little about some of the most important minerals.

Calcium
Needed daily for normal growth and particularly for healthy bones and teeth, a healthy heart and for other healthy muscles. *Source:* Milk and dairy products such as cheese, yoghurt, fromage frais; green vegetables such as kale and parsley; seeds.

Copper
Necessary for production of blood. Also involved in the healing process. *Source:* Green vegetables, potatoes, carrots. It is most unlikely that you will ever have too much.

Iodine
Necessary for healthy thyroid gland, which regulates body weight. Prevents premature ageing. *Source:* Watercress, fish, kelp, garlic. Normally present in table salt as it is added during the processing.

Iron
Necessary for production of red blood cells. Increases resistance to disease and stress. *Source:* Liver, beef, egg yolk, cereals, green vegetables, apricots.

Phosphorus
Works with calcium for healthy bones and teeth, etc. Essential for nerves. *Source:* Cheese, oatmeal, liver, kidney, carrots and dark green vegetables.

Potassium
Important because it acts as an alkaliser for acid-alkaline balance. Essential for muscle contraction and for nerve functions. Helps kidneys eliminate salt from the body. *Source:* Garlic, onions, mustard powder, cabbage.

Zinc
Necessary for healthy skin, for rebuilding cells. Vital for hormone and enzyme activities, especially reproduction. Helps to prevent painful joints. *Source:* Nuts, fish, leafy green vegetables, carrots and parsley.

JUICING FOR HEALTH AND VITALITY
Fruits and vegetables are great body cleansers. They are full of vitamins, minerals, enzymes and water, the most essential nutrient. We could all survive for a few weeks without food, but after two or three days without water, almost all humans would be dead. The body needs a constant supply of water and we get about 50 per cent of our fluid from food. Green vegetables, for example, are more than 90 per cent water.

Fruits and vegetables, particularly in the form of easily absorbed juice, provide the body with a wealth of benefits: they help our skin, nails and hair and make us look younger, they assist the brain and nervous system and stop us feeling depressed. They assist the internal organs to function correctly; they help our reproductive organs.

Common ailments
We all suffer from niggly common ailments from time to time such as colds, cold sores, insomnia, constipation etc.,

caused by a variety of things. Most of us see them as something we have to learn to put up with, or maybe pop into the chemist for advice.

Juices can help many of these ailments simply by providing the body with natural substances (vitamins and minerals) that will help counteract the symptoms. There are specific ailments that can be helped with fruit and vegetable juices. You will find that by taking a glass of juice made from ingredients containing the necessary minerals and vitamins you may considerably help the complaint by giving the body a terrific boost.

A host of old country legends exist surrounding remedies derived from herbs and plants: parsley, for instance, is said to be an excellent stimulant and a diuretic when taken in fairly large quantities. There are many examples of fruit and vegetables being used to combat ailments, proved continually and continuously to work, so dip into the following pages, reach for the juicer instead of the medicine cabinet and see how juice can act as a natural bottle of tonic. Should symptoms continue, it is, of course, advisable to consult your doctor.

Aching bones, stiff joints
The skeleton works pretty hard for us, so repay it with plenty of calcium. Vegetables with plenty of calcium include dark green varieties such as watercress, broccoli and parsley; mix them with something more palatable like carrot, apple and celery.

Cancer
It has been proved that fruit and vegetables with plenty of beta carotene, which the body converts into vitamin A, may help certain types of cancer. So drink cantaloupe juice, carrot and apple juice and juice made from all green vegetables with a little carrot, melon or apple to make them more palatable.

Colds and flu
Fruits and vegetables with high concentrations of vitamins A and C are excellent for warding off colds and flu. High doses of vitamin C over short periods will help you through the worst stages of a cold, so drink plenty of citrus juices (orange and grapefruit juice is great). Carrot with apple or

melon is also good; remember to juice melon with the skin on.

Constipation
Eat plenty of whole fruits and vegetables, unpeeled where possible. Drink almost any of the vegetable juice recipes and have one glass of black grape juice a day. Don't resort to taking laxatives; the body will sort itself out quite quickly the natural way.

Eyes
Sore, itchy eyes can be helped by vitamin A. Try any juice containing carrot or leafy green vegetables; this is particularly useful for hay fever sufferers when the pollen count is high. Try apricot and melon juice as well.

Flaking nails
Calcium is necessary for healthy bones, teeth and nails, so treat flaking, chipping nails from the inside by taking juice that's rich in calcium. This means dark green vegetable juice, so try broccoli with carrot and apple and any juice containing watercress. Cucumber with tomatoes and parsley is delicious too. Continue to drink these juice combinations daily over a two-week period and see your nails become healthier and stronger.

Hangovers and lethargy (general tiredness)
'The morning after the night before' hits us all at some time or another; alcohol has sapped the body of essential vitamins and minerals and left us feeling definitely one degree under and almost certainly dehydrated too.

Satisfy that raging thirst with plenty of water and healthy juice. Orange juice on its own is a great reviver first thing in the morning and will inject plenty of vitamin C into the system. Later in the day try melon with strawberry and good old carrot juice with watercress or cucumber. Drink as much juice as you feel you need on these days – up to six glasses a day. If possible take more vegetable than fruit juice.

Healthy gums and teeth
Unhealthy teeth and gums are all too common, and usually result from a diet that is too high in sugar. Drink juice such

as watercress with tomato, apricot with blackcurrant, carrot and celery with parsley. Persuade children not to drink sugary drinks and encourage everyone to brush their teeth after meals.

Indigestion and acid stomach
Try sipping juice with apple and carrot in it, even if you don't feel much like it; another good combination to soothe tummy ache is grape and pear. Indigestion sufferers should try juice containing parsley, onion and garlic in small quantities, which help the gastric juices.

Insomnia
Most of us suffer from insomnia at some time during our lives, often for no apparent reason. A glass of carrot and apple juice, taken on retiring, may help you to sleep through the night. Another good one is strawberry, melon and pear.

Lowering cholesterol
With heart disease claiming an alarming number of lives in the UK, many of us are becoming aware of the need to reduce the cholesterol level in our blood. What better way than by reducing our fat intake? Simply drink juice instead of eating a biscuit or a piece of cake. A glass of carrot juice with a little onion or garlic and apple will provide a satisfying snack that is exceptionally good for you. Tomato juice with carrot and red pepper is another winner. Carrot juice tastes surprisingly sweet, especially when combined with apple, so it immediately satisfies any cravings for sweet things.

Migraine and other headaches
A thumping headache is pretty awful to put up with at any time, so choose a soothing juice that doesn't taste sweet to nurse it better. Try celery with tomato and parsley: four stalks of celery with two tomatoes and a handful of parsley will give you about 250ml (8fl oz). Cucumber with pineapple is another option.

Nervous tension and anxiety
We all worry about various events in our lives. When your luck's down try a glass of strawberry and melon juice or

green grape with pear; hopefully, it will lift your spirits and make the problem a little smaller!

Skin problems
Encourage teenagers to drink carrot with apple or celery juice in place of squash as vitamin C really does help to clear the skin and combat acne and eczema. Try tomato juice with red pepper and carrot too. The effect will be noticed after about two weeks.

Sore throats
Plenty of soothing juice is wonderful when you have a sore throat; melon with pineapple is particularly good, and try tomato with celery and a little garlic or onion and parsley. Another good recipe is apple with apricot. Juice does seem to get to the spot; try four or five glasses a day and get plenty of rest.

Stress
Guard against stress, make sure you get a good night's sleep, and try a glass of any juice containing melon or strawberries. Pineapple with pear is excellent too, and seems to have a calming effect on the mind.

Sunburn
Although everyone loves to have a healthy tan, sunbathing is not good for the skin and sunburn is pretty uncomfortable. Of course it helps to apply cooling after-sun lotions to the affected parts, but try treating the skin from the inside with a soothing juice. Carrot juice with plenty of vitamin A will help guard against sunburn; try watercress with celery and tomato, and melon and strawberry too.

Trying to give up smoking?
Yes, juicing can even help you stop reaching for the weed! Give the body plenty of vitamins A and C with calcium and the cravings for tobacco definitely ease. Try orange with apple, melon and cherry and grapefruit with pear. Juice is a wonderful, healthy alternative to cigarettes.

A word about fibre
Juices are wonderful healthy drinks, but they contain little fibre, which is vitally important to the diet. It is made up of

a number of complex substances, all of which are carbo-hydrates. Foods rich in fibre such as wholemeal bread, pasta, pulse vegetables, potatoes etc., also supply our bodies with vitamins and minerals and they are all low in fat. Fibre is particularly beneficial in a healthy diet as it gives us a full feeling and stops us eating too much of the more calorie laden foods; it also aids the function of the digestive system and helps to prevent constipation.

There are two types of fibre: soluble fibre is found in fairly high quantities in fruit and vegetables, especially in red kidney beans, baked beans etc., and also in oats and oat products. It is believed that soluble fibre may help to reduce the level of cholesterol in the blood.

Insoluble fibre soaks up liquids inside us and swells up. Found in wheat products like wholemeal flour and bread, and some breakfast cereals; also in fibrous vegetables like carrots and cauliflower. This useful substance creates the full feeling, so is beneficial to those trying to reduce food intake.

JUICING TO SLIM

It's a fact of life that if you eat more than you need you'll put on weight; eat slightly less than the body needs and you'll lose weight. Go one step further and use up a few more calories through physical exercise, at the same time as reducing consumption of food, and weight will be lost even faster.

Exercise is a great way to slim: not only is weight lost through regular exercise, but muscles are firmed up, improving overall appearance, and increasing vitality. Regular physical exercise sustained over a reasonable period, say one hour's brisk walking or twenty minutes' jogging, daily, also reduces stress.

Can juicing help a weight-loss campaign? There is no doubt that it can – quick and easy to prepare, healthy juice can be an absolute boon to dieters.

The key to successful dieting is to change eating habits and to sustain that change throughout life. Many people skip breakfast and by 11a.m. are starving. The body craves an instant remedy to calm the hunger pangs – surely two or three biscuits won't hurt or a small packet of peanuts? – and so the day goes on, with the calories consumed from snacks alarmingly high.

A woman in a sedentary job burns approximately 2,100 calories a day so should not exceed this number in food intake (a man doing a similar job will burn a few more, 2,350 calories).

So let's rethink our eating habits. The trick is to reverse them. Don't restrict food intake – this will be almost impossible over long periods and even if you rapidly lose half a stone within six months that weight will go back on as you gradually but surely revert to bad eating habits.

Learn about food value and calorie content and replace those foods with a high fat and sugar content with low calorie alternatives. Eat plenty of high fibre, low calorie fruit and vegetables and also plenty of wholemeal bread with a scraping of low fat spread and perhaps a little yeast extract spread. If you're really hungry, try and eat two apples and two raw carrots; you'll be full up long before you've finished and the calorie count is minimal, but eat one slice of calorie laden gateau and you will still have room for another fattening treat.

A drink to your health

Fresh juice is a healthy alternative to caffeine and alcohol and is quick and easy to prepare with a juicer. Fruit and vegetable juice tastes so good that it becomes a real treat and can be looked upon as a reward. A 250ml (8fl oz) tumbler of vegetable juice has only about 60 calories; the same amount of fruit juice has approximately 120 calories, but this varies according to the sweetness of the fruit.

Juice is sustaining and invigorating, so it can be drunk to satisfy a craving for a snack and calm the appetite. It takes quite a few moments to drink a glass of foamy carrot and apple juice that almost instantly gives a wonderful lift making you full of zest. The stomach feels full too.

Drinking five or six glasses of vegetable juice a day fills the stomach and therefore reduces the desire to eat other foods that are almost inevitably higher in calories. Fruit juice, however, has a higher calorie count, so drink it as a reward, having just one or two glasses daily.

Foods to avoid

Remember, fat is the dieter's enemy; it is loaded with calories and, unfortunately, comes carefully hidden in a variety of foods.

Cheese: Contains 105 calories per 25g (1oz), so choose reduced fat cheeses that are now readily available in supermarkets.

Cake: Less than half a small fairy cake provides 85 calories yet a whole juicy apple has only about 75 calories.

Alcohol: High in sugar and empty calories, it provides zero food value, so avoid it and drink juice instead.

Crisps and peanuts: Many people's favourite snacks, they are, unfortunately, death to any diet because of their high concentration of fat. A 25g (1oz) serving of peanuts will cost you 170 calories – and you won't get very many nuts.

Milk and cream: Avoid both or restrict intake to minimal quantities and obtain calcium from vegetables and juice instead. Whole milk and cream are very high in fat and, therefore, calories; try to use the reduced fat varieties now readily available.

Tips for healthy eating
* Eat unrestricted amounts of fruit and vegetables, unpeeled where possible.
* Eat plenty of pasta and rice with vegetable sauces instead of fatty meat and cream based toppings.
* Make more of fish, especially white fish which is low in calories. Oily fish is good and filling. Cook it under the grill, on the barbecue or in the microwave for a change.
* Make more of salads, combining three or four raw ingredients of ranging colours and textures for health and vitality, along with a little protein.
* Eat plenty of wholemeal bread, which is high in fibre, with low fat spreads. Or 'go continental' and eat it on its own with soups and salads or fish dishes – you won't miss the butter as good bread has a wonderful flavour all of its own.

A juicing dieter's day
Try and start the day with ten minutes' exercise before breakfast.

Breakfast

    1 150ml (5fl oz) glass of fruit juice: Orange and Grapefruit Juice (see page 43) or Pineapple and Grapefruit Sunburst (see page 47)

    2 slices from a large wholemeal loaf, toasted and spread with 15ml (1 tablespoon) low fat spread and yeast extract

OR

    1 slice from a large wholemeal loaf, toasted and spread with 15ml (1 tablespoon) low fat soft cheese

Snack meal

    1 150ml (5fl oz) glass of vegetable juice: Carrot and Red Apple Juice (see page 90) or Tomato Juice with Fresh Herbs (see page 88)

    1 large granary bap filled with 50g (2oz) drained tuna fish in brine and plenty of salad

    1 large apple

OR

    2 slices from a large wholemeal loaf filled with 1 hard boiled egg, chopped and mixed with 5ml (1 teaspoon) reduced calorie mayonnaise, mustard and cress

Main meal

    175g (6oz) cooked and cooled long grain brown rice, mixed with half a finely chopped onion, 5cm (2in) cucumber, diced, 50g (2oz) mushrooms, chopped, and 75g (3oz) lean cooked chicken breast, chopped, all tossed in the juice from 2 tomatoes with 15ml (1 tablespoon) fresh herbs and served with half a red pepper, oven roasted with 5ml (1 teaspoon) oil until tender. Large leaf salad.

    1 150ml (5fl oz) glass of fruit juice such as Melon Juice with Strawberries (see page 49)

OR

    1 small 175g (6oz) trout or fresh salmon steak, grilled or poached, 175g (6oz) boiled new potatoes in their skins, 75g (3oz) peas, a large helping of homemade coleslaw made from grated carrot and cabbage tossed with the juice of 1 orange and 5ml (1 teaspoon) reduced calorie mayonnaise

    2 scoops Tomato Sorbet (see page 138)

If hunger pangs strike during the day, or evening, sip any of the vegetable juice recipes given in this book. Tea, coffee and alcohol should be avoided, but if you must drink tea or coffee have it weak, with very little semi-skimmed milk and no sugar.

BUYING FRUIT AND VEGETABLES

As you're now going to need more of these healthy staples, it's a good idea to find a good source that may prove a little cheaper than the local supermarket. You may be lucky enough to live near a farm with a shop or a 'pick your own' policy. Otherwise, try local markets – another excellent source of reasonably priced fruit and veg – but do check for quality and wash the produce carefully before juicing, scrubbing clean root vegetables.

Attractive fruits and vegetables are now available throughout the year as produce is flown in from abroad when our season ends. This is a terrific boon to the shopper, who has come to expect quality goods to be available continuously.

Buy and use fresh vegetables frequently. They are at their best nutritionally when they look most attractive – plump, firm, colourful. They will keep in the refrigerator for a few days, but they should be cut and used as soon as possible, while still bursting with goodness. Never leave prepared fruit and vegetables soaking in water as the food value will rapidly dissipate into the water. This is particularly true of vitamin C, which is also destroyed by heat and lost rapidly on storage.

As well as using fruit and vegetables in juices, continue to include them in your diet. A good guide is to have five separate portions a day.

Is organic produce best?

Throughout the British Isles, approximately 95 per cent of all our fruits, grains and vegetables are sprayed with pesticides at least once, and often they are sprayed more than once. These sprays, used to kill off insects, weeds etc. and to prevent disease in plants, therefore ensuring as perfect a crop as possible, are now known to contain substances that may cause allergies, and, in time, more serious illnesses in humans.

Organic farming is becoming more and more popular. Foods, be they fruits, grains and vegetables, or live stock, are grown or reared on healthy soil, with the aid of natural fertilisers and without spraying. The resulting foods are, therefore, completely natural and free from any pesticide residue. Remember, though, that the fruit and vegetables may not be quite so perfectly formed and evenly sized as those that are more controlled.

Where possible, when purchasing fruits and vegetables, try and buy organic. It may be just a little more expensive but with large supermarkets now offering an increasing range, organic goods are becoming readily available. Like all things, supply will meet demand, so the more organic produce is requested, the quicker the prices will fall.

The recipes in this book are all about health so it obviously makes sense to start off with the healthiest ingredients possible. Make the effort to purchase organic produce from supermarkets; 'pick your own' from organic farms and buy from market stalls that obtain their goods from organic sources. In later life you may be particularly glad you did, so make a noise now and ask for organic produce.

FRUITS FOR JUICING
See at a glance the concentrated goodness in a glass of juice.

Apples
The age-old rhyme 'An apple a day keeps the doctor away' may be true, as apples have been proved to be packed with natural substances that deserve this reputation.

Undoubtedly, the fruit helps to lower the cholesterol level in the blood. A French doctor asked a group of thirty middle-aged men and women not to change their diet at all, except to eat two or three apples every day for a month. By the end of that month, the blood cholesterol level in 80 per cent of the group had been reduced – in half of them the drop was of more than 10 per cent.

Apples are good for diabetics as they seem to help control blood pressure and sugar levels. The fruit also keeps the brakes on insulin.

Research has shown that regular apple eaters seem to contract fewer colds and respiratory problems; in fact people who eat three apples a day did seem to be far healthier than those who didn't. It is important to eat the skin, where it is thought anti-cancer chemicals are found.

23

Buy firm apples without bruises; look for a good colour and unwrinkled skin. Apples store reasonably well in a plastic bag in the refrigerator. Buy little and often.

Apples juice well and the juice is delicious and refreshing. Use one or two apples with other, less palatable, ingredients for delicious juice and drink immediately as it loses its colour quickly when exposed to the air.

Apricots

These wonderful little fruits have a fairly short season, so make the most of them whilst they are around. Available from June to September; choose plump, fairly soft, sound fruits with a wonderful aroma. Keep them in plastic bags in the fridge, but use as soon as possible. Apricots are a good source of potassium and of iron. They contain a valuable amount of vitamin A. Juice apricots without the stones.

Bananas

Bananas do not juice well. Like avocado pears, they are too soft to go through the machine. However, nutritionally, bananas are very valuable so eat them whole or purée them in the blender, adding milk to make a delicious shake, or slice them and add to other fruit juices.

Buy bright yellow bananas that look plump and un-damaged. Do not refrigerate as the skins will turn black. Store bananas in a fruit bowl in a cool, airy room. Bananas are a valuable source of fibre, containing more than almost any other fruit. They also supply B vitamins and some vitamin C as well as carbohydrate.

Cherries

Cherries are delicious sweet fruits available from June to late August. The best varieties grown in the UK are the sweet White Heart and the Black Heart. Buy firm, bright, evenly coloured fruits with young green stems. Store them, if necessary, in plastic bags in the fridge. Sweet cherries are a useful source of vitamin C and of potassium. Darker cherries are a reasonable source of iron and all cherries are a good source of vitamin A. Remove the stone before juicing.

Grapefruit

These wonderful fruits, with skins ranging from bright yellow to pink, are an excellent source of vitamin C, calcium, phosphorus and potassium. They also contain some vitamin B. The sweetness varies considerably, with pink grapefruit such as Star Ruby tasting sweeter than the yellow varieties. Buy firm, bright, heavy fruits which will yield most juice. Store, uncovered in the chill compartment of the refrigerator, if necessary.

Grapefruit and orange juice is a wonderful tonic to anyone suffering from a heavy cold, thanks to the boost of vitamin C.

For juicing, remove the rind and about half the bitter pith, then slice the fruit to fit the juicer, discarding the pips. Some pith should be left on the fruit as it has good food value. Grapefruits mix well with other, sweeter fruits for juicing; try them with oranges, melons or strawberries.

Grapes

Grapes are available throughout summer and autumn in many varieties. They all bruise easily so care must be taken when handling. White and black grapes are available with and without pips; seedless varieties are best for juicing. Choose plump, fat fruits with a natural bloom and green stems, as they are young and fresh. These stems may be juiced, but discard hard brown stems.

Grapes have a reasonable vitamin C content, a little vitamin B and also contain some potassium and iron. Grapes may be stored, if really necessary, in polythene bags with ventilating holes.

Kiwi fruit

Also known as Chinese gooseberries, these brown, furry, egg-shaped fruits are available most of the year round. Look for large, heavy fruits that are slightly soft. Kiwi fruits may be stored for a short time, uncovered, in the chill drawer of the refrigerator. They are excellent nutritionally, being a terrific source of vitamin C and also containing potassium. To juice, slice the whole fruit to fit the juicer.

Lemons

Lemons should be bright yellow, heavy and have a firm textured skin. Avoid dry looking fruits. Lemons are a valuable source of vitamin C but, as they taste rather acid, are best juiced with other sweeter fruits. A slice of lemon will give excellent flavour and zing to juice.

Lemons are now available all the year round. Store them, if necessary, in the chill compartment of the refrigerator. Peel before juicing then cut to fit the juicer.

Limes

Green limes are readily available all year round. Look for firm, heavy fruit with glossy, healthy skins. Limes are an excellent source of vitamin C. These wonderfully flavoured fruits should be used sparingly as, like lemons, they are rather acid to the palate. Try a slice of lime juiced with tomatoes and use rings of lime to decorate glasses of juice. Store, if necessary, in the chill compartment of the refrigerator. Peel before juicing.

Mangoes

These large tropical fruits vary considerably in size and colour. They have a wonderfully distinctive spicy, peachy flavour and the colour of the skin ranges from green to yellow and red. Ripe mangoes are slightly soft to the touch. Choose good coloured, reddish orange skins for juicing. Mangoes are an excellent source of vitamins A and C, and of B vitamins and potassium.

Store mangoes, if necessary, wrapped in the chill compartment of the refrigerator. Peel before juicing and discard the central stone.

Melons

Melons are available for most of the year, but are at their best during the summer and autumn months. Juicing captures all the goodness in the skin as well as the flesh. Look for firm, heavy fruit with a good colour and aroma.

All melons are excellent for juicing. Simply slice into pieces that will fit the juicer. Melons are a good source of vitamin C, folate and potassium. Water melon juice is particularly cool and refreshing.

Store melons, if necessary, in the chill compartment of the refrigerator.

Nectarines

Nectarines are the fruit of a type of peach tree. They have highly coloured, smooth skins, rather like plums, and a taste between a plum and a peach. Available throughout the summer months; look for large, heavy fruits that will juice well. Nectarines are a good source of vitamin C, and contain some vitamin B and potassium.

Store in the chill compartment of the refrigerator. Juice the fruit by cutting into slices, first discarding the central stone.

Oranges
Available all the year round, but cheapest in February and March. Select firm oranges with fresh, not wrinkled, skins that feel heavy for their size as these will contain considerably more juice. All oranges, satsumas, tangerines, etc. can be juiced. Peel the fruit and remove most of the white pith, which tastes bitter. Cut into slices to fit the juicer.

Oranges are a wonderful source of vitamin C: one medium orange supplies more than twice the daily requirements of this vitamin. They are also a good source of folic acid and dietary fibre and contain some potassium and vitamin B.

Juice made from oranges is far superior to supermarket orange juice, both nutritionally and in taste; just juice three or four oranges and taste the difference! Store oranges in the chill drawer of the refrigerator.

Peaches
Most of our peaches are imported from Italy, France and California and are readily available during the summer months. Select firm peaches of a good colour and leave to ripen for a day or two in the fruit bowl. The succulent flesh of a fresh, ripe peach has a wonderful flavour and aroma; they are juicy, refreshing and delicious.

Peaches are a reasonable source of vitamin C and carotene, with some B vitamin and potassium. Store ripe peaches, which bruise very easily, in the chill compartment of the refrigerator. Slice peaches to fit the juicer, discarding the central stone.

Pears
There are many dessert varieties of pears available, cultivated in many parts of the world. Some are particularly sweet and juicy when fully ripe, with a good flavour, so are excellent for juicing. They are available throughout the

summer and autumn, though English pears are fully ripe in late August and September and have a particularly good flavour. Supermarkets nearly always sell hard pears as they do not bruise. Keep them in a drawer for a day or two, ensuring that they don't touch each other. In two or three days they will change colour from green to yellow/pink and the flesh will become soft. Sweet, juicy pears are a good source of B vitamins with some vitamin C. They also contain phosphorus and calcium.

For juicing, select pears that are just ripe, not over-ripe, as the soft flesh can cause problems and clog up the juicer. It does help to juice pears with something a little harder, like carrots or apples.

Pineapples
This sweet aromatic tropical fruit has a wonderful deep orangey skin and firm, juicy, yellow flesh. There are many varieties which vary in size and colour. Buy fresh looking pineapples that are heavy for their size with healthy looking spines. Avoid any that look damaged or dry – they will be woody and unpleasant.

Pineapples are a wonderful source of vitamin C, carotene and the minerals phosphorus, magnesium, calcium and iron, so drink pineapple juice as often as you can.

To juice a pineapple, cut the cleaned fruit into rounds, about 5cm (2in) thick. (It's best to scrub the skin first under cold running water.) Discard the spine at the top of the pineapple, then cut the rounds into strips to fit the juicer. You may find it best to juice pineapple strips interspersed with orange or grapefruit segments to prevent the machine becoming clogged. The flavour is delicious too.

Plums
There are numerous varieties of plums grown throughout the world, ranging in colour from pale golden to red or very dark purple. The size varies too, from medium to large. Plums are a good source of carbohydrate and carotene with phosphorus and calcium. Store in the chill compartment of the refrigerator.

To juice plums, simply halve and discard the central stone. They are good juiced with other fruits. Apple and plum, pineapple and plum, and orange and plum are all delicious combinations.

Raspberries

These juicy, pink fruits are now widely cultivated. They vary in colour from red to yellow and are at their peak in late June and July. The full flavour of raspberries is best captured if they are juiced soon after picking. However, they freeze well at their peak and are an excellent standby in winter months when fresh fruit is difficult to come by. To freeze, lay sound clean fruit out on a tray and open freeze, then bag up and label.

Select firm, dry fruit for juicing that is as clean as possible. Rich, deep pink coloured raspberries tend to be sweetest and juice the best. Juice the fruit including the hulls. Try raspberries with other sweeter fruits such as peaches, pineapples, apples or strawberries.

Raspberries are an excellent source of vitamin C, containing useful quantities of iron, potassium and magnesium. They are, of all fruits, one of the best sources of dietary fibre, so eat them whole as well as juicing them.

Redcurrants and Blackcurrants

Redcurrants and blackcurrants are the fruits of bushes widely cultivated in the UK. Both grow in clusters and are in season from June to September. Blackcurrants are sharper to the palate and best juiced in small quantities with other sweet fruits.

Currants are a valuable source of vitamin C and also contain calcium, magnesium, phosphorus and iron. Buy them as fresh as possible – from a pick-your-own farm if there is one near you. Look out for plump, firm, brightly coloured berries without any sign of mildew. Store in a sealed bag in the refrigerator, if necessary. Currants freeze well.

Strawberries

Sweet succulent red fruits thAt grow close to the ground. Large, perfect, bright scarlet berries have a good flavour and juice well. Unlike raspberries, strawberries are not suitable for freezing.

Strawberries are an excellent source of vitamin C and carbohydrate; they are also fairly high in potassium and iron. Select fresh firm fruit with that wonderful strawberry aroma. If possible, pick your own at a fruit farm and wash and juice them straight away. As strawberry juice is rather thick on its own, it may be preferable to juice strawberries with other fruits. Watermelon and strawberry, apple and strawberry, orange and strawberry are all delicious combinations.

If strawberries must be stored, put them, in their punnet, into a polythene bag. Do not seal the bag. Keep them in the chill compartment of the refrigerator for one or two days only.

Tomatoes

Although often classed as a vegetable, this soft, pulpy fruit with a number of seeds is wonderful juiced on its own or with other fruits or vegetables. Try tomato and apple juice or tomato with carrot or celery. Look for ripe, firm, plump tomatoes with a distinct tomato aroma and a good red colour. Nutritionally tomatoes are a wonderful source of vitamins C, A and E. They store fairly well in the chill compartment of the refrigerator, but like all fruits and vegetables, are best consumed fresh. To juice, simply slice to fit the juicer.

VEGETABLES FOR JUICING

Vegetable juice is bursting with health and vitality and doesn't contain the fairly high amounts of sugar found in some fruit juices. If, for any medical reason, you have been advised to exclude certain vegetables from your diet, don't take them in concentrated juice form.

Vegetable juice is pretty strong stuff, so be sensible and drink only what your body tells you to. Juice derived solely from green vegetables should be avoided – it's too strong and doesn't taste very pleasant, so begin by following the recipes for vegetable juices in this book. You will find green vegetables mixed with other vegetables and sometimes fruits to make them more palatable. When you have become used to the balance, try your own recipes. Remember to wash thoroughly or scrub clean all the vegetables before juicing.

Bean sprouts

Buy crisp, fresh bean sprouts. They give a delicious Chinese flavour to juice. Store, in bags, in the chill compartment of the refrigerator for one to two days only. Bean sprouts are a great source of vitamin C.

Beans

If you grow fresh beans or broad beans in the garden, they are delicious juiced, mixed with other fruits or vegetables. Look for long, firm, healthy beans that snap crisply. Store, if necessary, in the refrigerator in a vented polythene bag. Green beans are an excellent source of vitamin C.

Beetroot

Blood red beetroots are good for you. Rich in iron, calcium and potassium, beetroots are also a valuable source of vitamins A and C. Beetroot is a good source of fibre so use it in salads or serve it as a hot vegetable for a change.

A small amount of beetroot only should be juiced with other fruits and vegetables for its nutritional properties. Try half a small beetroot to four carrots or four tomatoes with a half handful of parsley. Look for small, young, brightly coloured beetroots. Store, if necessary, in vented polythene bags in the chill drawer of the refrigerator.

Broccoli

Healthy, dark green broccoli with tight flower heads contains plenty of beta-carotene, vitamins B and C and also calcium, so do juice broccoli along with other ingredients. Avoid broccoli that has any yellow on it. Store in the chill compartment of the refrigerator if absolutely necessary. Cut to fit the juicer.

Brussels sprouts

Available in the autumn and winter months, sprouts should be of a uniform pale green colour. The heads should be tight. High in vitamin C and calcium as well as potassium, brussels sprouts also have a fairly good vitamin A content. Store sprouts in the chill compartment of the refrigerator. Juice with other vegetables or fruits.

Cabbage

There are many varieties of cabbage – white, red and green – available throughout the year. It is a plentiful, cheap vegetable and a valuable source of vitamins B and A, with some potassium, iron and calcium and variable amounts of vitamin C.

Look for fresh, firm, round heads whose outer leaves are of a deep colour; don't buy limp cabbage that has started to turn yellow. Cut into pieces to fit the juicer or roll individual leaves before juicing.

Carrots

Wonderful bright orange carrot juice is simply delicious mixed with a little celery or apple. It tastes like nothing you've ever tasted before!

Carrots have been available in Europe since Elizabethan times and can be bought throughout the year. They have a delicious sweet flavour and are an excellent source of carotene (vitamin A) with some vitamin B, calcium, iron and phosphorus.

Look for bright orange, fresh looking carrots and store, if necessary, in the chill compartment of the refrigerator. Carrots may be juiced on their own, or with other vegetables or fruits. Do not top or peel before juicing.

Cauliflower

Available in the autumn and winter months, the cauliflower is a member of the cabbage family. Look for firm, close curds or 'flowers', protected by firm green leaves. Cauliflower is a good source of vitamin C and of the B vitamins, as well as folate, potassium and some vitamin K. Use cauliflower with other vegetables and fruits to make palatable, nutritious juices. Cauliflower may be stored, if necessary, in the chill compartment of the refrigerator. Cut into pieces to fit the juicer.

Celery

A vegetable of the carrot family, celery is available all the year round although English celery, grown from October to March, is deemed to have the best flavour.

Celery stalks contain natural sodium that helps maintain body fluids as well as vitamin C and potassium. The juice is refreshing and cleansing as it is a natural diuretic. Drink celery juice on its own or mixed with other fruits or vegetables.

Look for firm, crisp heads of celery with healthy leaves. Store in the chill compartment of the refrigerator or stand, in the refrigerator, in a jug containing 5cm (2in) of cold water.

Courgettes

Summer courgettes are young and tender with a delicious flavour. Similar in nutrients to cucumbers, courgette juice also acts as a natural diuretic. Mix small, firm courgettes with tomatoes and parsley or carrot or celery for refreshing palatable juices.

Store courgettes in the chill compartment of the refrigerator if necessary.

Cucumbers

The saying 'As cool as a cucumber' is so apt: cucumbers keep cool all on their own and are comprised largely of water. They juice well and are best mixed with other ingredients to produce palatable juice. Choose firm, dark green, straight cucumbers, avoiding those which have marks or bruises. They contain potassium and act as a natural diuretic.

Fennel

Florence fennel is the swollen stem of the plant we buy and use as a vegetable. It is often used sliced in salads or lightly boiled and served with a cheese sauce. All of the plant has a distinctive aniseed flavour.

Look for firm, creamy white fennel with feathery green tops. Avoid any that are wilted or look dry. Fennel is a reasonable source of vitamin C with some potassium and vitamin B. Mix with other vegetables and fruits such as apple, carrot, tomato or celery.

Store, if necessary, in the chill compartment of the refrigerator.

Garlic

Garlic has had a vast amount of publicity recently as a cure for all ills! It has been around for centuries and over the years has become famous for its healing properties. It is good for digestion and has been proved to aid in ridding the body of cholesterol.

Juice one clove of garlic per glass of juice; there's no need to peel it. It will give excellent flavour to carrot, apple or tomato and parsley juice. One clove of garlic, per person, per day is normally sufficient.

Each garlic bulb is a collection of several small bulbs or cloves, bound together by a papery skin. Look for firm tight bulbs with no sign of mildew or decay and store at room temperature.

Ginger
Ginger comes from the underground root of a tropical plant and has a pleasant odour and spicy taste. Try juicing a piece of ginger, about 2.5cm (1in) long, with apple or pear or tomato and carrot juice. The flavour is subtle and delicious. Ginger is particularly good for the mucous membranes and for anyone suffering from catarrh.

Lettuce
There are many varieties of lettuce, which was first introduced into Britain in the sixteenth century. Choose from Little Gem, Butterhead, Lakeland, Roquette, Lollo Rosso, Cos or Oak Leaf to name but a few.

Lettuce is largely comprised of water, but is rich in vitamin A with some vitamin C. It acts as a natural body cleanser. Look for bright firm heads of lettuce with healthy leaves. Store in the chill compartment of the refrigerator, if necessary, in sealed plastic bags. Lettuce juice is unpalatable on its own, so mix it with carrot, tomato or apple juice.

Mushrooms
Mushrooms are now available all the year round, but are at their best in summer and autumn. Look for firm mushrooms, heavy for their size, with a good colour, according to their variety, and a pleasant smell. Avoid dry-looking mushrooms. There are many varieties of mushroom, some of which grow wild in fields during the summer and autumn – pick them only if you are absolutely certain that you can identify edible mushrooms.

Mushrooms have a delicate flavour and are a good source of the B group of vitamins and of potassium. Use them with tomato and parsley or with celery and apple.

Onions (including spring onions)
This type of bulb is widely grown throughout the world and is available all the year round. Look for firm, healthy onions with tight skins. Add a little onion when juicing carrots or

tomatoes with peppers; they give good flavour if the juice is to be used in a savoury dish. Onions contain some vitamin C and minerals.

Do not keep onions in the fridge as they tend to taint other foods. Store them for short periods, in the vegetable rack.

Peppers
These attractive, fluted, bell-shaped vegetables are the fruits of the capsicum plant. Readily available all year round, the shiny skins vary in colour from green to yellow and from orange to red depending on the ripeness and the variety. Look for well-shaped, firm peppers with deep colours. They are rich in vitamins A and C with some potassium. Store, if necessary, in the chill compartment of the refrigerator.

Potatoes
Potatoes are highly nutritional vegetables: they are a good source of carbohydrate with excellent amounts of vitamin C, also vitamin B, calcium and iron. For this reason it is worth adding one or two when juicing carrots or watercress and tomato. Choose fresh, firm potatoes and discard any that have green patches which can be poisonous.

Store potatoes in a cool, dry place – the vegetable rack in a coolish kitchen is fine. Buy and use potatoes often in preference to storing them.

Radishes
Like onions, radishes should be juiced in small quantities as their rather peppery taste is quite strong. Look for firm, bright red radishes that look healthy. Add a little radish to tomatoes or carrots when juicing them to add a peppery kick that's very pleasant.

Radishes supply a reasonable amount of vitamin C and some potassium and sodium and can be stored, if necessary, in plastic bags in the chill compartment of the refrigerator.

Spinach
Dark green spinach is a good source of vitamins A and C and of iron. Spinach is also an excellent body cleanser as it flushes through the system, taking waste products with it.

Choose bright green, healthy leaves with no signs of

yellow or of wilting. Well washed spinach can be stored, if necessary, in the chill compartment of the refrigerator. Spinach tends to be very dirty and gritty, so it is very important to wash it in several changes of water before using. Roll leaves up before juicing and use with other vegetables such as carrots or celery and tomato or apple.

Watercress
Watercress, as the name suggests, grows in water. Commercially grown watercress is now available all the year round. The leaves have a pleasant peppery taste, not unlike radish, and watercress is a useful source of vitamins A and C, and of iron and calcium. Look for fresh, healthy leaves with no sign of yellowing.

Wash watercress particularly well before juicing with celery or apple, or tomato and carrot. Watercress juice on its own is not very pleasant, so don't try it!

HERBS FOR JUICING
Fresh cut herbs are wonderful with all sorts of foods and will enhance and add flavour to many of your super juice recipes. Herbs are pretty in the garden and emit a deliciously fresh aroma, especially after a shower of rain. If you don't have a garden, you may prefer to grow herbs in pots on the window sill. Alternatively, an outdoor bowl, about 45cm (18in) in diameter, doesn't take up much space and will provide room for about seven different types of herbs.

Try adding chopped mixed herbs the next time you roast a chicken: simply sprinkle them over the breast and legs, then wrap loosely in foil and roast as usual.

A little chopped basil is delicious on pizza, and try adding snipped chives and chopped parsley to fish next time you have a barbecue.

Basil
This herb has distinctive bright green flat leaves with pointed ends. Basil is often served with tomato recipes as it complements the flavour so well. Try it with fish and pasta dishes too. The smaller leaves make a pretty garnish.

Chives
Resembling long grass, chives have pale pink flowers in June which are excellent in salads. Chives are chopped

quickly with scissors and have a distinct onion flavour. Use sparingly in dressings and soups. Good with cheese dishes.

Coriander
Also known as flat leaved or Chinese parsley. Although coriander looks like a flat leaved parsley, it tastes very different; it has a strong lemony flavour which is particularly good in Indian cookery. Try it in chicken tikka and tandoori chicken. Add a little, finely chopped, to the next mixed salad you prepare.

Coriander seeds have a mild orange flavour. Use crushed in meat balls, shepherd's pie and curry sauces for a delicious flavour.

Garlic
Garlic, although hated by some (it can always be left out of a recipe), gives the most wonderful flavour to home cooking and is very easy to grow in the garden – just plant a few cloves about 5cm (2in) apart in early spring, water them well and by August you will have your own crop of delicious fresh garlic.

Lemon balm
Also known as sweet balm, this herb is very fragrant and has a distinct lemon flavour. Try the finely chopped leaves in stuffings, jam recipes, fruit salads, vegetable salads and in drinks. The attractive leaves are also useful as a garnish on savoury dishes and as a decoration on ice creams and desserts.

Marjoram
Gold-tipped marjoram is a hardy perennial herb, with attractive gold-tipped leaves. This herb has rose purple flowers in July. Use marjoram leaves, finely chopped, for flavouring soups and stews; it is also good in omelettes and quiches. The plant attracts bees and butterflies.

Mint
Available in a wide range of varieties but spearmint is the one most widely used in cooking. Excellent in juice and in lots of recipes, both sweet and savoury. Use the leaves, finely chopped, in salads and salad dressings; add a few sprigs when boiling new potatoes. A few tiny leaves add

piquancy to fruit punches and can also be used as a decoration on desserts such as summer pudding, ice creams and sorbets.

Oregano
This sweet aromatic herb is a wild marjoram; a bushy herb of the mint family. Excellent in Italian dishes such as pizza, pasta dishes, meat sauces, etc. Try it in salad dressings and stuffings for poultry. Oregano is good dried.

Parsley
Parsley is the most widely used of all herbs. The leaves are used, finely chopped, to enhance all sorts of cooking and are excellent as a garnish. The stalks can be added to stock and are also good, finely chopped, in stuffings. Parsley butter is wonderful on new potatoes or steamed carrots. Parsley acts as a natural diuretic and is a reasonable source of vitamin C.

Rosemary
With its needle-like leaves and strong, woody flavour, rosemary is delicious with lamb and pork dishes and excellent laid on the barbecue where it will quickly fill the air with a pungent aroma. Rosemary grows into quite a large bush and you use scissors to cut off sprigs for kitchen use. Try adding a couple of sprigs when you marinate fish.

Thyme
Thyme, with its pretty deep-pink flowers, is often found growing wild. A bush of thyme in the garden will provide fresh leaves all the year round. Quite strongly flavoured, a little fresh thyme goes a long way. Use finely chopped, or add a sprig or two next time you grill steak or pork chops for a pungent aroma and delicious flavour.

HINTS FOR SUPER JUICING
1. *Do* stir the juice before serving and drink the froth, as much of the goodness is contained in it. Some manufacturers supply machines that have a special anti-froth baffle that strains the juice as you pour, thus giving a clear juice that children may prefer.
2. *Do* use a plastic spatula to help empty the hopper.
3. *Do* ensure the machine is assembled correctly, with the jug in place, before you start to juice. Juicing without

the jug in position will send juice all over the machine and the kitchen!

4. *Don't* attempt to juice aubergines, avocados, bananas, blackberries or figs as machines can't cope with the texture. Similarly, overripe fruits.

5. *Do* juice herbs with other ingredients containing plenty of water such as carrots, tomatoes, etc., adding them in the middle of the juice operation.

6. *Do* limit your consumption of fruit juice, which is high in natural sugar, particularly if a doctor has recommended restricting your sugar intake.

7. *Do* drink vegetable juice freely – it's filling so it's great for slimmers. However, it may cause wind initially, so experiment with different combinations; carrot with celery, parsley and a little apple is wonderful.

8. *Do* peel grapefruit, oranges and mangoes and remove any hard brown stems from grapes before juicing. Remove pips from citrus fruit as they can make the juice bitter.

9. *Do* be aware that tough skinned fruits and vegetables such as pineapple and onion can cause problems in juicing. Remove these skins before juicing if they seem to block the juicer, and stop the machine to clean off the filter if the machine starts to sound sluggish. Scrub clean all root vegetables.

10. *Do* wash well all fruits and vegetables before juicing.

Fruit Juices

Orange and Grapefruit Juice

This sunny juice is ideal for breakfast or at any time of the day when you want a refreshing drink.

Serves 4

2 large oranges
1 large grapefruit

To serve
150ml (5fl oz) sparking mineral water, chilled
slices of orange (optional)
slices of lime

1. Peel the oranges and grapefruit, leaving about half the pith on the fruit.
2. Cut fruit into slices and discard the pips. Store in a mixing bowl as you prepare.
3. With the motor running, extract juice from the fruit. Stir well.
4. Divide between four wine glasses. Top up with the chilled mineral water and serve immediately, garnished with the slices of orange and lime.

This recipe makes approximately 375ml (13fl oz) concentrated juice.

Pineapple, Raspberry and Apple Cooler

Like something from a Caribbean island, this drink makes you think you're sitting in the sunshine, wherever you are!

Serves 2 to 3

1 5cm (2in) thick slice from a fresh pineapple, including skin
2 Granny Smith apples
100 g (4oz) raspberries

To serve
ice cubes (optional)
sprigs of fresh mint

1. Cut the pineapple ring into strips so it will fit easily into the juicer. Store in a mixing bowl.
2. Slice apples and put into bowl with the raspberries.
3. With the motor running, extract juice from the pineapple, apples and raspberries. Stir well.
4. Place ice cubes in two or three wine glasses. Pour juice over and serve immediately. Decorate with the sprigs of mint.

This recipe makes approximately 450ml (15fl oz) concentrated juice.

Black Grape and Kiwi Juice

This delicious fresh tasting juice is a wonderful pick-me-up when you're feeling rather jaded. Grapes contain potassium and some iron, which is vitally important for healthy blood. An excellent juice for anyone who suffers from constipation. To make crushed ice, place ice cubes within a strong polythene bag and crush with a rolling pin.

Serves 2

350g (12oz) black grapes, including green stems
1 kiwi fruit

To serve
crushed ice
slices of lemon

1. Cut kiwi fruit into four segments and put with grapes in a mixing bowl, snipping the grapes into manageable bunches and discarding any thick brown stems.
2. With the motor running, extract juice from the grapes and kiwi fruit. Stir well.
3. Put some crushed ice into two wine glasses. Pour over juice and serve immediately. Decorate with slices of lemon.

This recipe makes approximately 250ml (8fl oz) concentrated juice.

Apple-ade

A simple combination of two common fruits that works brilliantly. Buy heavy oranges and other citrus fruits as they'll have the most juice.

Serves 3

4 apples
2 oranges

To serve
crushed ice
slices of orange

1. Cut apples into slices to fit the juicer.
2. Peel the oranges, removing about half the pith.
3. Cut each orange into segments and remove pips.
4. With the motor running, extract juice from the apples and oranges. Stir well.
5. Divide crushed ice between three wine glasses. Pour juice over the ice and serve immediately, garnished with slices of orange.

This recipe makes approximately 350ml (12fl oz) concentrated juice.

Pineapple and Grapefruit Sunburst

Any drink based on citrus fruits is particularly refreshing and a good source of vitamin C too. As with all the juices, this should be drunk as soon as it is prepared.

Serves 3

1 5cm (2in) thick slice from a fresh pineapple, including skin
1 pink grapefruit (Star Ruby if possible)
1 pear

To serve
ice cubes (optional)
slices of cucumber

1. Cut the pineapple ring into strips so it will fit easily into the juicer. Store in a mixing bowl.
2. Peel the grapefruit, leaving about half the pith on the fruit. Cut into segments that will fit the juicer, discarding the pips. Add to bowl.
3. Cut pear into juiceable slices. Add to bowl.
4. With the motor running, extract juice from the prepared fruit. Stir well.
5. Place ice cubes in three wine glasses. Top up with juice and serve immediately, garnished with slices of cucumber.

This recipe makes approximately 400ml (14fl oz) concentrated juice.

Green Grape and Apple Juice

Drink this one for a boost when you're feeling a little tired. Young children love it as it's sweet, although, if you find it too sweet, it can be diluted with mineral water. (Not suitable for anyone who shouldn't consume too much sugar, such as diabetics.)

Serves 4

4 Granny Smith apples
350g (12oz) green grapes, including green stems

To serve
crushed ice
sprigs of fresh mint

1. Slice the apples into juiceable pieces and assemble with the grapes in a mixing bowl, snipping the grapes into manageable bunches and discarding any thick brown stems.
2. With the motor running, extract juice from the grapes and apples. Stir well.
3. Put some crushed ice into four wine glasses. Pour the juice over the ice and serve immediately. Decorate with the sprigs of mint.

This recipe makes approximately 600ml (1 pint) concentrated juice.

Melon Juice with Strawberries

Honeydew melons, skin and all, make perfect juice as they contain quite a large amount of water. The flavour of this summer cooler is out of this world – try it on a hot, sticky afternoon.

Serves 3

½ honeydew melon, with seeds and skin
100g (4oz) strawberries
1 large peach

To serve
ice cubes
slices of lime

1. Cut melon into thin slices to fit the juicer. Store in a mixing bowl.
2. Halve the strawberries if necessary and put in the bowl. Slice peach, discarding central stone, and add to the bowl.
3. With the motor running, extract juice from the melon, strawberries and peach. Stir well.
4. Divide between three wine glasses, add ice and a lime garnish on serving.

This recipe makes approximately 475ml (16fl oz) concentrated juice.

Cantaloupe Juice

Ripe cantaloupes smell sweet and appetising and are delicious juiced entirely on their own. Try them as a change from citrus juice at breakfast.

Serves 2

½ cantaloupe melon

To serve
crushed ice (optional)

1. Cut melon into thin slices that will fit the juicer.
2. With the motor running, extract juice from the melon. Stir well.
3. Put a little crushed ice into two wine glasses. Pour the melon juice over the ice and serve immediately.

This recipe makes approximately 300ml (½ pint) concentrated juice.

Strawberry and Kiwi Juice

Sweet, refreshing and bursting with vitamin C, the whole family will love this foamy refresher that is so full of goodness.

Serves 4

350 g (12oz) strawberries
4 kiwi fruit

To serve
crushed ice (optional)

1. Put strawberries into a mixing bowl, halving if necessary.
2. Cut kiwi fruit into slices and add to the bowl.
3. With the motor running, extract juice from the strawberries and kiwi fruit. Stir well.
4. Put a little crushed ice into four wine glasses.
5. Pour the juice on to the ice and serve immediately.

This recipe makes approximately 600ml (1 pint) concentrated juice.

Summer Blush

This juice tastes as good as it looks. Strawberries have an excellent vitamin C content and juice well; kiwi fruit and peach add a delicious flavour. Serve with or without ice for a refreshing summertime drink.

Serves 2

2 kiwi fruit
1 peach
100g (4oz) strawberries

To serve
crushed ice
sprigs of fresh mint

1. Slice the kiwi fruit to fit the juicer.
2. Halve the peach and discard the central stone. Slice peach halves to fit the juicer.
3. With the motor running, extract juice from the kiwi fruit, peach and strawberries. Stir well.
4. Divide crushed ice between two wine glasses.
5. Pour juice over the ice and serve immediately. Decorate with the sprigs of mint.

This recipe makes approximately 300ml (½ pint) concentrated juice.

Three-Fruit Quencher

A refreshing drink for a hot day. Good with ice and a sprig of
cool apple mint.

Serves 2

2 large oranges
1 Granny Smith apple
100g (4oz) ripe green grapes, including green stems

To serve
ice cubes
sprigs of fresh apple mint

1. Peel the oranges leaving about half the pith on the fruit.
2. Cut oranges into slices that will fit the juicer. Discard pips
   and store oranges in a mixing bowl.
3. Cut apple into slices to fit the juicer. Store in a mixing
   bowl with the grapes.
4. With the motor running, extract juice from the prepared
   fruit. Stir well.
5. Place ice cubes in two tumblers. Top up with juice, then
   serve immediately with the apple mint.

This recipe makes approximately 300ml (½ pint) concentrated juice.

Tropical Dream

A delightful combination of flavours that's simply delicious, and a favourite with adults when served as a dessert with ice cream. It can also be served as an aperitif diluted with a little sparkling mineral water or sparkling wine.

Serves 3

1 grapefruit
1 orange
1 kiwi fruit
100g (4oz) green grapes, including green stems

To serve
ice cream (optional)

1. Peel the grapefruit and orange, leaving about half the pith on.
2. Cut grapefruit and orange into slices that will fit the juicer. Discard the pips. Store fruit in a mixing bowl. Slice the kiwi fruit and add to the bowl. Add the grapes, discarding any brown stems.
3. With the motor running, extract juice from the prepared fruits. Stir well.
4. Serve in wine glasses, with a scoop of ice cream, if using.

This recipe makes approximately 450ml (15fl oz) concentrated juice.

Juice Dessert

Wonderfully sweet and creamy, this delicious drink makes a dessert in a glass.

Serves 2

225g (8oz) strawberries
1 orange
1 pear

To serve
ice cubes
sprigs of fresh mint

1. Cut the strawberries to fit the juicer and store in a bowl.
2. Peel the orange, leaving about half the pith on, and discard the pips. Add to the mixing bowl.
3. Slice the pear and put in the bowl.
4. With the motor running, extract juice from the fruit. Stir well.
5. Pour into wine glasses and serve with ice cubes and sprigs of mint.

This recipe makes approximately 300ml (½ pint) concentrated juice.

Healthy Breakfast Juice

Start the day with a 'zingy' fruit drink packed with vitamins and minerals. Use any type of melon in this juice.

Serves 2

½ grapefruit
1 orange
1 150g (5oz) slice melon

To serve
ice cubes

1. Peel and slice the grapefruit and orange leaving on about half the pith. Discard the pips, and assemble the fruit in a large mixing bowl.
2. Slice the melon to fit the juicer. Add to the bowl.
3. With the motor running, extract juice from the fruit. Stir well.
4. Put ice cubes into two wine glasses and add the juice. Serve immediately.

This recipe makes approximately 300ml (½ pint) concentrated juice.

Melon and Nectarine Juice

Melons juice very well and, combined with sweet nectarines, make a refreshing, tasty juice that's an excellent summer cooler.

Serves 2

1 150g (5oz) slice melon
2 ripe nectarines

To serve
ice cubes

1. Slice the melon to fit juicer and store in a mixing bowl.
2. Cut nectarines in half, remove the stones and slice to fit juicer. Put into the mixing bowl with the melon.
3. With the motor running, juice the melon and nectarines. Stir juice well.
4. Divide the ice between two tumblers, top up with juice and serve immediately.

This recipe makes approximately 300ml (½ pint) concentrated juice.

Strawberry Cocktail

A rich, thick, fruity drink that can be topped up with mineral water or lemonade if desired.

Serves 2

6 medium size strawberries
100g (4oz) grapes, with green stems
2 apples

To serve
crushed ice

1. Halve strawberries, if necessary, and store in a mixing bowl.
2. Remove any brown stems from the grapes and put the fruit in the bowl.
3. Cut apples into juiceable slices and add to the other prepared fruit.
4. With the motor running, juice strawberries, grapes and apples. Stir juice well.
5. Divide ice between two tumblers, top up with juice and serve immediately.

This recipe makes approximately 300ml (½ pint) concentrated juice.

Tomato and Nectarine Juice

Tomatoes, although normally used as a vegetable, are classified as a fruit and have a fresh, somewhat sweet flavour that combines well with nectarines to create a refreshing juice.

Serves 2

5 medium size tomatoes
1 nectarine
½ apple

To serve
ice cubes

1. Cut tomatoes into wedges to fit the juicer. Store in a large mixing bowl.
2. Halve the nectarine, discard the stone, then slice each half to fit the juicer. Add to the bowl.
3. Slice the apple to fit the juicer and also add to the bowl.
4. With the motor running, juice the tomatoes, nectarine and apple. Stir juice well.
5. Divide ice cubes between two tumblers, top up with juice and serve immediately.

Makes approximately 275ml (9fl oz) concentrated juice.

Apple and Kiwi Reviver

Fresh crisp apples combine well with kiwi fruit in a clean-tasting juice that is a good pre-dinner drink. Serve with ice and a slice of lime.

Serves 2

3 Granny Smith apples
2 kiwi fruit

To serve
ice cubes
slices of fresh lime

1. Cut apples and kiwi fruit into slices to fit the juicer. Store in a mixing bowl beside the juicing machine.
2. With the motor running, juice the prepared fruit. Stir well.
3. Divide the ice between two tumblers, top up with juice and serve immediately. Decorate with a slice of lime.

This recipe makes approximately 450ml (15fl oz) concentrated juice.

Watermelon Cooler

Watermelon needs nothing added as it makes a most refreshing and cool drink all on its own. Remember to juice all of the melon, including skin and pips, for maximum benefit and taste and don't worry about the colour!

Serves 2

1 400g (14oz) slice watermelon

1. Cut the watermelon into slices to fit the juicer.
2. With the motor running, juice the watermelon. Stir well.
3. Divide between two tumblers and serve immediately.

This recipe makes approximately 350ml (12fl oz) concentrated juice.

Grapefruit and Nectarine Bomb

A delicious tangy drink to make your taste buds tingle. Serve it for breakfast or as an afternoon reviver. A thick and creamy juice that's also good with a little mineral water.

Serves 2

1 grapefruit
1 nectarine
1 small peach

To serve
ice cubes

1. Remove the peel and about half the pith from the grapefruit, then cut the fruit into slices to fit the juicer and store in a mixing bowl.
2. Cut the nectarine into juiceable slices, discarding the central stone, and add to the bowl.
3. Cut the peach into slices to fit the juicer, discarding the central stone, and place with the other fruit.
4. With the motor running, juice the grapefruit with the nectarine and the peach. Stir well.
5. Put ice cubes into two tumblers, add the juice and serve immediately.

This recipe makes approximately 300ml (½ pint) concentrated juice.

Peach, Orange and Cucumber Cooler

A juice that will always be cool: cucumbers remain naturally cold to the touch even on a summer's day.

Serves 2

1 large peach
2 medium size oranges
½ cucumber

1. Cut the peach in half, discarding stone, then slice the halves to fit the juicer. Store in a mixing bowl.
2. Peel the oranges, discarding about half of the pith. Divide into juiceable slices, discarding the pips. Add to the bowl.
3. Cut the cucumber to fit the juicer and place in the bowl.
4. With the motor running, juice the peach, orange and cucumber. Stir juice well.
5. Divide between two tumblers and serve immediately.

This recipe makes approximately 300ml (½ pint) concentrated juice.

Redcurrant and Melon Juice

Choose plump, bright redcurrants bursting with vitamin C, that are naturally sweet.

Serves 2

225g (8oz) Ogen melon
100g (4oz) redcurrants

1. Cut the melon into juiceable pieces and store in a bowl with the redcurrants for easy handling.
2. With the motor running, juice the melon and redcurrants. Stir juice well.
3. Pour into two wine glasses and serve immediately.

This recipe makes approximately 300ml (½ pint) concentrated juice.

Pear, Apple and Ginger Juice

Ginger gives apples and pears a warming, comforting flavour. Try this 'moreish' fruity juice on a winter's evening.

Serves 2

1 Cox's Orange Pippin or Granny Smith apple
2 large pears
1 2.5cm (1in) piece root ginger

1. Cut apples and pears into juiceable slices.
2. Cut ginger to fit the juicer, if necessary.
3. With the motor running, juice the apples with the pears and the ginger. Stir the juice well.
4. Divide between two tumblers and serve immediately.

This recipe makes approximately 300ml (½ pint) concentrated juice.

Pineapple and Apricot Crush

Pineapple is a wonderful remedy for sore throats, so drink as much as you can to ward them off. Top up this thick juice with a little sparkling mineral water and serve with ice for a refreshing, healthy tonic.

Serves 2

1 5cm (2in) slice pineapple
2 apricots

To serve
150ml (5fl oz) sparkling mineral water
ice cubes

1. Cut the pineapple into pieces to fit the juicer. Store in a mixing bowl.
2. Halve the apricots, discarding the stones, then cut into slices to fit the juicer and place with the pineapple in the mixing bowl.
3. With the motor running, juice the pineapple and apricots. Stir the juice well and add the mineral water.
4. Divide the ice between two tumblers, top up with juice and serve immediately.

This recipe makes approximately 275ml (9fl oz) concentrated juice.

Orange and Pineapple Zing

A simple combination that tastes wonderful and will instantly transport you to that tropical island. Try it once and you'll make it often.

Serves 2 to 3

1 5cm (2in) slice pineapple
2 large oranges

To serve
ice cubes

1. Cut the pineapple into slices to fit the juicer and store in a mixing bowl.
2. Peel the oranges, removing about half the pith.
3. Slice the orange flesh to fit the juicer, discarding the pips, and place in the mixing bowl with the pineapple.
4. With the motor running, juice the fruit. Stir the juice well.
5. Divide the ice between the tumblers, add the juice and serve immediately.

This recipe makes approximately 350ml (12fl oz) concentrated juice.

Tropical Trio

Ripe, juicy mangoes are rich in vitamin A and C and in potassium. They have a distinctive flavour that mixes well with cool kiwi fruit and tangy pineapple in this exotic fruit cocktail.

Serves 2

1 mango, peeled
1 kiwi fruit
1 5cm (2in) slice pineapple

To serve
ice cubes

1. Slice the mango into pieces to fit the juicer, discarding the central stone. Store the flesh in a mixing bowl.
2. Cut the kiwi fruit into slices to fit the juicer and add to the bowl.
3. Cut the pineapple into juiceable strips and place in the bowl.
4. With the motor running, juice the mango, kiwi and pineapple. Stir the juice well.
5. Divide the ice cubes between two tumblers, pour in the juice and serve immediately.

This recipe makes approximately 250ml (8fl oz) concentrated juice.

Peach Juice

Juice made from sun-ripened juicy peaches, with their enticing aroma, is thick and sweet. Peaches are also a useful source of vitamin B3 and vitamin A. Try this juice mixed with a little sparkling lemonade, served with ice.

Serves 2

3 large peaches
150ml (5fl oz) sparkling lemonade

To serve
ice cubes

1. Halve the peaches, discarding the central stone, and cut each half into slices to fit the juicer.
2. With the motor running, juice the peaches. Stir the juice, adding the lemonade.
3. Divide the ice cubes between two tumblers, pour in the juice and serve immediately.

This recipe makes approximately 300ml (½ pint) concentrated juice.

Nectarine and Redcurrant Juice

Serve this pretty, summery juice at any time for a refreshing drink that provides plenty of vitamin C.

Serves 2

3 large nectarines
100g (4oz) redcurrants

1. Halve the nectarines, discarding the central stone, then cut each half into slices to fit the juicer. Store in a bowl with the redcurrants.
2. With the motor running, juice the nectarines and redcurrants. Stir the juice well.
3. Divide the juice between two wine glasses and serve immediately.

This recipe makes approximately 250ml (8fl oz) concentrated juice.

Blackcurrant and Pear Juice

Blackcurrants are an excellent source of vitamin C. The juice on its own is somewhat sour but mixed with sweet ripe pears it's a winner.

Serves 2

2 large pears
100g (4oz) blackcurrants

To serve
ice cubes
sprigs of fresh mint

1. Cut the pears into juiceable slices and put in a bowl with the blackcurrants.
2. With the motor running, juice the pears and black-currants. Stir the juice well.
3. Divide the ice cubes between two tumblers, top up with juice and serve immediately, adding a sprig of mint to each glass.

This recipe makes approximately 250ml (8fl oz) concentrated juice.

Raspberry and Apple Juice

Rich juicy raspberries are a reasonable source of vitamin C, and they also taste sweet and fruity. Try this delicious combination of raspberries with apples that makes a refreshing drink for two.

Serves 2

3 Granny Smith or Cox's Orange Pippin apples
100g (4oz) raspberries

To serve
ice cubes

1. Slice the apples to fit the juicer and store in a bowl with the raspberries.
2. With the motor running, juice the apples with the raspberries. Stir the juice well.
3. Divide the ice cubes between two wine glasses, top up with the juice and serve immediately.

This recipe makes approximately 350ml (12fl oz) concentrated juice.

Melon and Pineapple Juice

Refreshing, cool melon with tangy pineapple is a super combination of flavours. Serve this juice with ice for a refreshing drink that everyone will love.

Serves 2

½ canteloupe melon
1 baby pineapple

To serve
ice cubes
slices of cucumber

1. Cut the melon into slices and place in a mixing bowl.
2. Remove and discard the spiky leaves of the pineapple then cut into slices that will fit the juicer.
3. With the motor running, juice the melon and pineapple. Stir the juice well.
4. Divide the ice cubes between two wine glasses, pour in the juice and serve immediately. Decorate with the cucumber slices.

This recipe makes approximately 450ml (15fl oz) concentrated juice.

Grapefruit and Strawberry Crush

One sip of this glorious pink drink will convert you to juicing, without a doubt. Full of vitamin C and vitality, it's a delicious breakfast drink.

Serves 2

1 pink grapefruit
100g (4oz) strawberries

To serve
ice cubes

1. Peel grapefruit, removing about half of the pith.
2. Cut the grapefruit into slices that will fit the juicer and store in a mixing bowl.
3. Halve strawberries, if necessary, and put in the bowl with the grapefruit.
4. With the motor running, juice the grapefruit and the strawberries. Stir the juice well.
5. Put ice into two wine glasses, top up with the juice and serve immediately.

This recipe makes approximately 300ml (½ pint) concentrated juice.

Red Grape and Apple Juice

This attractive and refreshing juice is also fairly sustaining due to the natural sweetness in the juice. You may like to serve it on ice, topped up with a little mineral water.

Serves 2

175g (6oz) seedless red grapes, brown stems removed
3 Cox's Orange Pippin apples

To serve
ice cubes

1. Divide the grapes into small bunches that will fit the juicer and store in a bowl.
2. Slice the apples to fit the juicer and add to the bowl.
3. With the motor running, juice the grapes and apples. Stir the juice well.
4. Divide the ice cubes between two wine glasses, top up with the juice and serve immediately.

This recipe makes approximately 350ml (12fl oz) concentrated juice.

Cherry, Peach and Cucumber Cooler

When fresh cherries are available, use them in juice; they're full of vitamins and minerals and are very juicy. The sweetness of the cherries and peach is wonderful combined with the bland cucumber. This juice will be naturally cool so is excellent served on a hot sticky summer's day.

Serves 3

225g (8oz) dark red cherries, stoned
2 peaches
½ cucumber

To serve
sprigs of fresh mint

1. Put the washed, stoned cherries into a bowl beside the juicer.
2. Slice the peaches, discarding the central stone, and add to the bowl.
3. Cut the cucumber to fit the juicer and store in the bowl.
4. With the motor running, juice the cherries with the peach and cucumber.
5. Divide between three wine glasses and serve immediately.

This recipe makes approximately 550ml (18fl oz) concentrated juice.

Note: When fresh ripe cherries aren't available, use black or white seedless grapes instead.

Pear and Apricot Fizz

The subtle combination of pear with apricot is simply delicious. The apricot season is short so make the most of it and serve this refreshing drink often. A thick, sweet, fruity juice.

Serves 3

3 large apricots, halved and stoned
2 large pears
150ml (5fl oz) sparkling lemonade or mineral water

To serve
crushed ice
fresh cherries

1. Cut apricots into narrow slices and store in a mixing bowl.
2. Cut pears into slices and add to the bowl.
3. With the motor running, extract juice from the apricots and pears. Stir well.
4. Put a little crushed ice into three tumblers.
5. Divide juice between the glasses. Top each glass up with lemonade or mineral water and stir before serving. Decorate with the fresh cherries.

This recipe makes approximately 550ml (18fl oz) concentrated juice.

Honeydew Fizz

Red grapes and melon are delicious together and the mineral water adds a pleasantly refreshing fizz to the drink.

Serves 6 punch glasses

1 honeydew melon, cut to fit juicer
225g (8oz) red grapes, dark brown stems discarded
150ml (5fl oz) sparkling mineral water

To serve
sprigs of fresh mint
slices of cucumber
ice cubes

1. Juice the melon and grapes.
2. Pour the juice into a punch bowl.
3. Add the mineral water with the mint and cucumber.
4. Serve immediately, with ice.

This recipe makes approximately 1 litre (1¾ pints).

Strawberry Fizz Punch

A wonderfully fruity punch with an optional kick from the orange-flavoured liqueur. Fruit-based wines are available from most large supermarkets; they are low in alcohol and pleasantly sparkling.

Serves 10 punch glasses

450g (1lb) strawberries, cut to fit juicer
1 wedge lemon, peeled and sliced to fit juicer
25g (1oz) icing sugar
85ml (3fl oz) Grand Marnier (optional)
1 75cl bottle strawberry fruit wine, chilled

1. Slice six strawberries and reserve for decoration.
2. Assemble lemon and remaining strawberries in a large bowl beside the juicer. Juice the fruits.
3. Transfer juice to a punch bowl and stir in the icing sugar with the Grand Marnier.
4. Add the strawberry fruit wine and reserved strawberries and serve immediately.

This recipe makes approximately 1.5 litres (2½ pints).

Mid-summer Punch

A wonderfully refreshing non-alcoholic punch to serve on a summer evening. Always extremely popular, so be prepared to double the recipe!

Serves 6 punch glasses

2 large oranges, peeled and sliced to fit juicer, discarding pips
1 large pink grapefruit, peeled and sliced to fit juicer, discarding pips
1 5cm (2in) slice pineapple, sliced to fit juicer
1 5cm (2in) piece cucumber, sliced to fit juicer
300ml (½ pint) lemonade

To serve
sprigs of fresh mint
slices of orange, quartered
ice cubes

1. Store all the fruit with the cucumber in a large mixing bowl as you prepare it.
2. Juice the fruit in the juicer, with the cucumber, then transfer to a punch bowl. Stir well.
3. Add the lemonade, sprigs of mint, orange slices and ice cubes and serve immediately.

This recipe makes approximately 1 litre (1¾ pints).

Coconut Pineapple Punch

The juicer produces wonderful coconut cream. Try this tropical recipe which is delicious with ice.

Serves 6 punch glasses

½ coconut, peeled and flesh cut to fit juicer
1 medium size pineapple, sliced to fit juicer
85ml (3fl oz) Bacardi rum (optional)
500ml (17fl oz) soda water, chilled

To serve
ice cubes
sprigs of fresh mint

1. Place coconut flesh and pineapple in a large mixing bowl beside the juicer.
2. Juice the fruit. Transfer to a punch bowl and stir in the Bacardi, if using.
3. Just before serving add soda water, ice and sprigs of mint.

This recipe makes approximately 1 litre (1¾ pints).

Fruit Ice Cubes

These pretty ice cubes will enhance all the fruit juices and, as
the ice melts, you are left with the whole fruit which is
delicious to eat. Try a similar theme using fresh herbs for the
vegetable juices, it works just as well. Sprigs of mint and
parsley, a few chives, etc. would be ideal.

You will need one large, fairly deep ice cube tray.

sprigs of redcurrants and blackcurrants
a few raspberries
still mineral water

1. Leaving the stalks on the currants and the hulls on the
   raspberries, divide them between the ice cube compart-
   ments, putting about five currants or a raspberry into
   each.
2. Top up with water, fairly carefully.
3. Freeze until solid.
4. Serve with fruity juices.

Vegetable Juices

Carrot and Courgette Juice

This delicious pick-me-up is thinner than carrot juice on its own. The combination of carrot with the sweet apple and rather earthy courgette is particularly refreshing.

Serves 4

6 carrots, topped
2 courgettes
1 Red Delicious apple
3 sprigs coriander
½ handful fresh parsley

To serve
ice cubes (optional)

1. Cut carrots and courgettes into juiceable pieces, and store them in a mixing bowl.
2. Slice the apple and add to the bowl.
3. With the motor running, extract juice from carrots, courgettes, apple, coriander and parsley. Stir well.
4. Serve in wine glasses, with ice if desired.

This recipe makes approximately 475ml (16fl oz) concentrated juice.

Herby Carrot Juice

The stick of celery gives this carrot juice a delicious flavour; organic celery tastes best. Best served with ice cubes.

Serves 3

1 small potato
8 medium size carrots
1 stick celery
1 handful fresh herbs (parsley, thyme, mint, oregano, etc.)

To serve
ice cubes (optional)

1. Cut potato, carrots and celery into juiceable pieces and store in a mixing bowl.
2. With the motor running, extract the juice from the vegetables and fresh herbs.
3. Stir the juice well and serve immediately with ice cubes.

This recipe makes approximately 350ml (12fl oz) concentrated juice.

Tomato and Orange Juice

The slight sweetness in oranges is delicious with tomato juice. Jugs of this juice are great for summer barbecues – it looks very attractive too.

Serves 3

6 medium size tomatoes
1 large orange
½ handful fresh basil

To serve
crushed ice
freshly chopped chives

1. Slice each tomato into juiceable pieces and store in a mixing bowl.
2. Peel the orange, leaving half the pith on the fruit. Cut into 6 segments and discard the pips. Add to the bowl.
3. With the motor running, extract juice from the tomatoes and orange, with the basil added. Stir the juice well.
4. Put some crushed ice into three wine glasses. Pour out the juice and serve immediately, garnished with the snipped chives.

This recipe makes approximately 450ml (15fl oz) concentrated juice.

Tomato Juice with Fresh Herbs

Coriander combines well with tomatoes, but it is a fairly pungent herb. Use only a little, with other herbs such as chives, parsley, basil and sage, in this drink.

Serves 3

6 medium size tomatoes
1 lemon slice
1 handful mixed fresh herbs

To serve
crushed ice
freshly chopped chives

1. Slice each tomato into juiceable pieces and store in a mixing bowl.
2. With the motor running, extract juice from the tomatoes and the slice of lemon, with the herbs. Stir the juice well.
3. Put some crushed ice into three wine glasses, pour in the juice and serve immediately. Garnish with the chopped chives.

This recipe makes approximately 350ml (12fl oz) concentrated juice.

Radish and Celery Juice with Pear

Radishes need to be juiced with something sweet to make them more palatable. Celery and pear are just the thing and will create a drink that's a real tonic.

Serves 3 to 4

2 pears
3 radishes
2 sticks celery

1. Slice the pears into juiceable pieces and store in a mixing bowl.
2. Add the washed radishes to the bowl.
3. Roughly chop the celery and add this to the bowl.
4. With the motor running, extract the juice from the pears, radish and celery. Stir the juice well.
5. Serve immediately in wine glasses.

This recipe makes approximately 475ml (16fl oz) concentrated juice.

Carrot and Red Apple Juice

The superb flavour of Red Delicious apples is wonderfully earthy with sweet carrots. Try this juice at 4p.m. instead of the usual cup of tea for a real lift.

Serves 3 to 4

6 carrots
2 Red Delicious apples

To serve
ice cubes (optional)

1. Cut the carrots into juiceable pieces. Store in a mixing bowl.
2. Slice the apples and add to the bowl.
3. With the motor running, extract juice from the carrots and apples. Stir the juice well.
4. Put ice cubes into each of the wine glasses. Add the juice and serve immediately.

This recipe makes approximately 450ml (15fl oz) concentrated juice.

Tomato Refresher

Bean sprouts are readily available in supermarkets. They juice well and give a Chinese feel to this healthy drink that is the most fantastic colour: it looks rather like a witch's brew!

Serves 1

75g (3oz) bean sprouts, organically grown if possible
2 medium size tomatoes
½ raw beetroot, including top

1. Put the washed bean sprouts into a mixing bowl.
2. Slice the tomatoes to fit the juicer and add to the bowl.
3. With the motor running, juice the bean sprouts with the tomatoes and well washed beetroot. Stir the juice well.
4. Pour into a wine glass and serve immediately.

This recipe makes approximately 200ml (7fl oz) concentrated juice.

Parsnip, Celery and Carrot Juice

This filling and delicious juice is a real aid to dieters: try it mid-morning or during the evening when hunger pangs strike.

Serves 2 to 3

2 medium parsnips
2 medium carrots
2 large celery stalks
4 sprigs celery leaves
1 apple

To serve
ice cubes
chopped chives

1. Cut the parsnips, carrots and celery into pieces to fit the juicer and assemble in a mixing bowl near the juicing machine.
2. Slice the apple to fit the juicer and add to the bowl.
3. With the motor running, extract juice from the parsnips, carrots, celery, celery leaves and apple. Stir well.
4. Serve with ice, sprinkled with the chives.

This recipe makes approximately 450ml (15fl oz) concentrated juice.

Apple Beet Juice

Beetroot is rich in iron and calcium and makes a delicious juice cocktail when mixed with apples and celery.

Serves 2

2 apples
2 sticks celery
½ small beetroot
½ handful celery leaves

1. Cut apples, celery and well-washed beetroot into juiceable pieces and store in a bowl with the celery leaves.
2. With the motor running, juice all the ingredients. Stir the juice well.
3. Serve immediately in two tumblers.

This recipe makes approximately 300ml (½ pint) concentrated juice.

Carrot Beet Juice

Blood-red beetroot is good for you and tastes great when mixed with other vegetables or fruits.

Serves 1

½ small beetroot
4 carrots
½ handful fresh basil

To serve
ice cubes

1. Cut the well washed beetroot and well scrubbed carrots into pieces to fit the juicer and store in a bowl. Add the basil.
2. With the motor running, juice the beetroot, carrots and basil. Stir the juice well.
3. Serve in a tumbler with the ice cubes.

This recipe makes approximately 175ml (6fl oz) concentrated juice.

3 Cs Juice

This healthy juice is delicious served with plenty of ice on a hot summer's day.

Serves 2

½ medium cauliflower
½ cucumber
10 cherries
½ apple

To serve
ice cubes

1. Cut the cauliflower and cucumber into pieces to fit the juicer and store in a mixing bowl.
2. Stone the cherries and cut the apple into slices. Add to the bowl.
3. With the motor running, juice the cauliflower, cucumber, cherries and apple. Stir the juice well.
4. Divide the ice cubes between the tumblers, add the juice, and serve immediately.

This recipe makes approximately 450ml (15fl oz) concentrated juice.

Cucumber and Pineapple Plus

You can actually feel this refreshing juice doing you good!
The cool cucumber combines well with the sweet pineapple
and the sprig of mint adds a summery flavour.

Serves 2

1 5cm (2in) pineapple round
1 7.5cm (3in) piece cucumber
2 sprigs fresh mint

To serve
ice cubes

1. Cut the pineapple and cucumber into juiceable pieces.
2. With the motor running, juice the pineapple and cucumber with the mint. Stir the juice well.
3. Divide the ice cubes between the two tumblers, top up
   with juice and serve immediately.

This recipe makes approximately 250ml (8fl oz) concentrated
juice.

Carrot, Pepper and Parsley Juice

There's plenty of vitamin A in this tasty juice, which is also very filling. Ideal for weight watchers.

Serves 2

6 carrots
225g (8oz) summer cabbage
½ red pepper
4 sprigs fresh parsley

To serve
ice cubes

1. Cut carrots, cabbage and pepper into juiceable pieces. Store in a bowl with the parsley beside the juicer.
2. With the motor running, juice all the ingredients. Stir well.
3. Divide the ice cubes between two tumblers, top up with juice and serve immediately.

This recipe makes approximately 300ml (½ pint) concentrated juice.

Carrot, Cauliflower and Basil Juice

This delicious juice is ideal for children who refuse to eat vegetables. You'll find they enjoy the combination of flavours if you don't mention what's in it!

Serves 2

4 carrots
5 cauliflower florets
1 apple
4 basil leaves

1. Cut the carrots, cauliflower and apple to fit the juicer and store in a large bowl with the basil.
2. With the motor running, juice the vegetables and apple with the basil. Stir the juice well.
3. Divide between two tumblers and serve.

This recipe makes approximately 250ml (8fl oz) concentrated juice.

Tomato, Courgette and Celery Juice

This juice is great for the skin and is also excellent for the eyesight. Drink it often as it's cheap to make and delicious.

Serves 2

4 large tomatoes
1 medium size courgette
1 stick celery
1 small lemon wedge
4 sprigs fresh parsley

1. Cut tomatoes, courgette and celery into pieces to fit the juicer. Store in a bowl with the lemon and parsley.
2. With the motor running, juice all the ingredients and stir well.
3. Divide between two tumblers and serve immediately.

This recipe makes approximately 300ml (½ pint) concentrated juice.

Tomato and Carrot Juice

This juice is a great reviver that helps combat colds and flus.

Serves 1

4 medium size carrots
3 medium size tomatoes
1 stick celery

To serve
ice cubes (optional)

1. Cut carrots, tomatoes and celery to fit the juicer and place in a bowl.
2. With the motor running, juice all the ingredients and stir well.
3. Serve in a tumbler, with ice if desired.

This recipe makes approximately 250ml (8fl oz) concentrated juice.

Vegetable Medley

A tangy vegetable cocktail livened up with a fresh Cox's apple. If you can't get Cox's, any other variety of eating apple will do for this great pre-lunch pick-me-up.

Serves 2

225g (8oz) summer cabbage
3 medium size carrots
1 Cox's Orange Pippin apple
3 broccoli florets

To serve
ice cubes

1. Cut the cabbage into pieces to fit the juicer and store in a mixing bowl.
2. Cut the carrots and apple into juiceable pieces and add to the bowl with the broccoli florets.
3. With the motor running, juice the cabbage, carrots, apple and broccoli. Stir the juice well.
4. Put ice cubes into two tumblers, top up with the juice and serve immediately.

This recipe makes approximately 350ml (12fl oz) concentrated juice.

Salad Harmony

A juice made from fresh salad vegetables with herbs that's full of garden goodness.

Serves 3

3 tomatoes
½ cucumber
1 medium size carrot
1 Worcester apple
1 Little Gem lettuce
1 spring onion
15ml (1 tablespoon) chopped chives
3 sprigs fresh parsley

1. Slice the tomatoes to fit the juicer and store in a bowl.
2. Cut the cucumber into lengths and add to the bowl.
3. Cut the carrot to fit the juicer and add this to the bowl.
4. Cut the apples into juiceable slices and add to the vegetables.
5. Cut the Little Gem lettuce into wedges to fit the juicer and put into the bowl, adding the spring onion, chopped chives and parsley.
6. With the motor running, juice all the ingredients. Stir the juice well.
7. Divide between three wine glasses and serve immediately.

This recipe makes approximately 450ml (15fl oz) concentrated juice.

Courgette, Carrot and Apple Juice

A juice that is excellent for blood circulation and for the mucous membranes. It will also act as a natural diuretic. Children will enjoy the mild flavours.

Serves 2 to 3

2 courgettes
2 carrots
1 apple

To serve
ice cubes

1. Cut the courgettes and carrots into pieces to fit the juicer. Store in a mixing bowl.
2. Slice the apples and add to the bowl.
3. With the motor running, juice the courgettes, carrots and apple then stir the juice well.
4. Divide the ice cubes between the tumblers, top up with juice and serve immediately.

This recipe makes approximately 450ml (15fl oz) concentrated juice.

Spinach Trio

Spinach with carrot and apple is a healthy trio if ever there was one. Enjoy this vegetable cocktail as a pre-dinner drink that makes you feel so good.

Serves 2

3 medium carrots
1 apple
6 spinach leaves, rolled
4 sprigs fresh parsley

1. Cut the carrots into pieces to fit the juicer and place them in a mixing bowl.
2. Slice the apple and add it to the bowl.
3. With the motor running, juice the carrots with the apple, spinach and parsley. Stir the juice well.
4. Divide the juice between two wine glasses and serve immediately.

This recipe makes approximately 300ml (½ pint) concentrated juice.

Spinach Cocktail

Spinach has plenty of vitamins A and C as well as iron. Try it in this recipe combined with Brussels sprouts, carrots, celery and flavoured with garlic.

Serves 2

3 medium size carrots
2 sticks celery
5cm (2in) piece cucumber
3 spinach leaves, rolled
6 Brussels sprouts
2 cloves garlic

1. Cut the carrots, celery and cucumber into pieces to fit the juicer. Place these with all the other ingredients into a mixing bowl.
2. With the motor running, juice the vegetables. Stir the juice well.
3. Divide between the two tumblers and serve immediately.

This recipe makes approximately 300ml (½ pint) concentrated juice.

Cucumber and Celery Juice

Cucumber with celery makes a deliciously cool and refreshing drink with plenty of vitamin B. This soothing juice is excellent for sore throats and helps promote healthy skin and eyes.

Serves 2

½ cucumber
2 sticks celery
1 clove garlic
4 sprigs fresh parsley

1. Cut the cucumber and celery into juiceable pieces and store with the other ingredients in a mixing bowl.
2. With the motor running, juice the cucumber, celery and garlic with the parsley. Stir the juice well.
3. Divide between two tumblers and serve immediately.

This recipe makes approximately 275ml (9fl oz) concentrated juice.

Radish and Apple Juice

Radishes, with their somewhat peppery taste, contain most of the B vitamins and some vitamin C, and they are a good source of iron, calcium and phosphorus. The apples make the juice sweeter, naturally, and therefore more enjoyable.

Serves 2

3 apples
6 radishes

To serve
ice cubes

1. Slice the apples to fit the juicer and put into a bowl with the radishes beside the juicing machine.
2. With the motor running, juice the apples and radishes. Stir the juice well.
3. Divide the ice cubes between two tumblers, pour in the juice and serve immediately.

This recipe makes approximately 300ml (½ pint) concentrated juice.

Pepper and Carrot Juice

Colourful peppers are full of vitamins, including A, B3, B6 and plenty of vitamin C. Carrots are simply bursting with goodness as they supply B vitamins, some vitamins C and E, and lots of calcium. So drink plenty of this healthy juice.

Serves 2

1 red pepper
1 yellow pepper
4 medium size carrots
4 sprigs fresh marjoram

To serve
ice cubes

1. Slice the red and yellow peppers to fit the juicer and store in a mixing bowl.
2. Cut carrots into juiceable pieces and add to the bowl.
3. With the motor running, juice the vegetables with the marjoram. Stir the juice well.
4. Divide the ice cubes between two tumblers, add the juice and serve immediately.

This recipe makes approximately 300ml (½ pint) concentrated juice.

Mixed Pepper Juice

Plenty of vitamins make pepper juice highly nutritious; the carrot makes the juice a little thicker and adds vitamin A.

Serves 2

1 green pepper
½ red pepper
½ yellow pepper
1 medium size carrot

To serve
ice cubes

1. Cut the peppers into juiceable slices and store in a mixing bowl.
2. Cut the carrot into pieces to fit the juicer and add to the bowl.
3. With the motor running, juice the pepper slices with the carrot. Stir the juice well.
4. Divide the ice cubes between two wine glasses, top up with juice and serve immediately.

This recipe makes approximately 275ml (9fl oz) concentrated juice.

Vegetable Mix I

A refreshing combination of vegetables that make a palatable juice.

Serves 2

3 medium carrots
1 tomato
100g (4oz) broccoli
6 spinach leaves, rolled

1. Cut carrots and tomato into juiceable pieces and store in a mixing bowl with the other ingredients.
2. With the motor running, juice the carrots with the tomato, broccoli and spinach leaves. Stir the juice well.
3. Pour into two tumblers and serve immediately.

This recipe makes approximately 350ml (12fl oz) concentrated juice.

Vegetable Mix II

A delicious filling mix of flavours that's ideal for weight watchers.

Serves 2

3 medium carrots
100g (4oz) cauliflower
100g (4oz) white cabbage
1 tomato
15ml (1 tablespoon) freshly chopped parsley

1. Cut carrots, cauliflower, cabbage and tomato into pieces that will fit the juicer. Store with the parsley in a bowl beside the juicing machine.
2. With the motor running, juice the carrots, cauliflower, cabbage and tomato with the parsley. Stir the juice well.
3. Pour juice into two wine glasses and serve immediately.

This recipe makes approximately 350ml (12fl oz) concentrated juice.

Carrot Bomber

Carrots are combined with radish, celery and healthy parsley in a juice that's great for slimmers – it's filling and revitalising. And what's more, carrots are absolutely delicious with celery.

Serves 1

2 medium carrots
2 large sticks celery
2 radishes
½ handful fresh parsley

To serve
ice cubes

1. Cut celery and carrots into juiceable pieces and place in a mixing bowl.
2. Halve the radishes, if necessary, and store in the bowl.
3. Juice the carrots, celery and radishes with the sprigs of parsley. Stir the juice well.
4. Serve in a tumbler with ice cubes.

This recipe makes approximately 150ml (5fl oz) concentrated juice.

Carrot and Cucumber Quencher

This orange-coloured drink is clean tasting and fairly sustaining. It's a real reviver after energetic sport.

Serves 2

4 medium carrots
1 small ridge cucumber
1 orange
3 sprigs fresh basil

To serve
ice cubes

1. Cut carrots and cucumber to fit the juicer. Store in a mixing bowl.
2. Peel the orange, removing about half the pith, then segment to fit the juicer, discarding the pips. Add the fruit to the bowl with the basil.
3. With the motor running, juice the carrots, cucumber, orange and basil. Stir the juice well.
4. Divide the ice cubes between two wine glasses, add the juice, and serve immediately.

This recipe makes approximately 300ml (½ pint) concentrated juice.

Summer Salad Juice

This refreshing juice will remind you of the summer months whatever time of year you choose to make it. Delicately flavoured with fennel and full of vitamins, it's good for adults and children.

Serves 2

2 medium size tomatoes
½ yellow pepper
1 7.5cm (3in) wedge Iceberg lettuce
½ medium bulb fennel
1 medium carrot

To serve
ice cubes (optional)

1. Slice the tomatoes to fit the juicer and store in a mixing bowl.
2. Cut the pepper to fit the juicer and add to the bowl.
3. Cut the lettuce, fennel and carrot into juiceable pieces and add to the bowl.
4. With the motor running, juice the tomatoes, pepper, lettuce, fennel and carrot. Stir the juice well.
5. Divide the ice cubes between two wine glasses, top up with juice and serve immediately.

This recipe makes approximately 300ml (½ pint) concentrated juice.

Green Bean Juice

Green beans with carrot and celery is a tonic in a glass that's filling as well, so drink it often when fresh green beans are available.

Serves 1

100g (4oz) green string beans
1 medium carrot
1 stick celery

To serve
ice cubes

1. Cut beans, carrot and celery into pieces to fit the juicer and store them in a bowl.
2. With the motor running, juice all the ingredients. Stir the juice well.
3. Put the ice cubes into a wine glass, top it up with juice and serve immediately.

This recipe makes approximately 175ml (6fl oz) concentrated juice.

Soups, Sauces and Marinades

These soups, sauces and marinades are quick and easy to make and tasty. Juicing is a real boon in cooking as there are so few ingredients to peel that preparation is kept down to a minimum. However, the main advantage is that all the flavour found just under the skin of fruits and vegetables is captured to give these recipes a fresh and delicious taste.

Family and friends will enjoy the tasty Marinated Chinese Chicken (see p. 133) and Pasta and Vegetable Soup with Beans (see p. 121), and you'll be amazed just how useful a juicer is, not only to make fruit and vegetable juices, but for quick and easy recipes too.

Gazpacho

This wonderful soup tastes fresh and healthy, particularly when served on warm summer evenings. It can also be packed into a thermos and taken on picnics, but some of the fragile vitamin C will be lost.

Serves 4

1 fat clove garlic, chopped
½ handful fresh parsley
4 medium size tomatoes, sliced to fit juicer
½ onion, sliced to fit juicer
3 carrots, topped and chopped to fit juicer
1 red pepper, de-seeded and sliced to fit juicer
1 10cm (4in) piece cucumber, sliced to fit juicer
30ml (2 tablespoons) red wine vinegar
A little sea salt and freshly ground black pepper

To serve
crushed ice
freshly chopped basil

1. With the motor running, extract juice from all the vegetables.
2. Stir well, adding vinegar and seasoning to taste.
3. Arrange a little crushed ice in four soup bowls.
4. Pour the gazpacho over the ice. Garnish with chopped basil and serve immediately.

This recipe makes approximately 650ml (22fl oz) gazpacho.

Red Lentil Soup

This filling soup has plenty of protein and the lentils provide carbohydrate, vitamins, iron and calcium. The juice adds a delicious fresh flavour to the soup, which is best served with chunks of wholemeal bread.

Serves 4

½ lemon, peeled and sliced to fit juicer
225g (8oz) tomatoes, sliced to fit juicer
1 medium size onion, sliced to fit juicer
1 clove garlic
1 handful fresh parsley
15ml (1 tablespoon) oil
2 rashers streaky bacon, chopped, with rind removed
225g (8oz) red lentils, washed
1 litre (1¾ pints) chicken or vegetable stock

To serve
30ml (2 tablespoons) freshly chopped basil

1. Juice the lemon with the tomatoes, onion, garlic and parsley. Set aside.
2. Heat the oil in a large saucepan then fry the bacon over a medium heat until just starting to crisp.
3. Add the lentils and stir to coat with oil. Add the juice from the juicer and the stock. Bring to the boil, then cover and simmer for 45 minutes, until the lentils are tender.
4. Transfer to a food processor and, using the metal blade, process until smooth. (This may need to be done in two batches.)
5. Re-heat to serving temperature, and serve sprinkled with the basil.

This recipe makes approximately 1.2 litres (2 pints) soup.

Pasta and Vegetable Soup with Beans

A filling soup that's quick and easy to prepare and full of food value. Serve piping hot with wholemeal rolls.

Serves 4

1 onion, sliced to fit juicer
2 sticks celery, chopped to fit juicer
2 carrots, cut to fit juicer
1 green pepper, sliced to fit juicer
25g (1oz) butter
25g (1oz) wholemeal flour
30ml (2 tablespoons) tomato purée
300ml (½ pint) vegetable stock
1 400g (14oz) can chopped tomatoes
1 430g (15oz) can red kidney beans, drained and rinsed
50g (2oz) spaghetti, broken into 3 lengths
Freshly ground black pepper

1. Juice the onion with the celery, carrots and green pepper and set aside.
2. Melt the butter in a large, heavy based pan.
3. Stir in the flour and cook, stirring for 1 minute.
4. Blend together the tomato purée and stock and add this to the pan with the can of tomatoes.
5. Stir in the juice from the juicer with the red kidney beans and the spaghetti. Add a seasoning of black pepper.
6. Bring to the boil, stirring, then cover and simmer for 15 minutes.
7. Serve immediately.

This recipe makes approximately 900ml (1½ pints) soup.

Special Apple Sauce

This refreshing apple sauce has all the taste of fruit plus the sweetness of the sultanas. Delicious with pork dishes, curries and burgers.

Serves 4

1 eating apple, sliced to fit juicer
1 large orange, peeled and sliced to fit juicer, discarding pips
450g (1lb) Bramley apples, peeled, cored and sliced
10ml (2 teaspoons) caster sugar
50g (2oz) sultanas

1. Assemble the apple and orange in a bowl, near the juicing machine, then juice them.
2. Put the Bramley apple slices into a large, heavy based saucepan. Add the sugar and the sultanas. Pour over the juice from the juicer.
3. Simmer, covered, for about 10 minutes, stirring occasionally, until the apples soften. Remove from heat and turn into a serving dish.
4. Serve the sauce warm or cold.

This recipe makes approximately 300ml (½ pint) sauce.

Tangy Orange and Herb Sauce

A sauce that's ideal to serve with fish and chicken dishes, especially spicy ones like tandoori or chicken tikka. It is also delicious eaten cold with salad and fish dishes.

Serves 4

150ml (5fl oz) natural yoghurt
1 orange, peeled and divided into segments, discarding pips
4 sprigs fresh parsley
2 basil leaves or 3 celery leaves
A little sea salt and freshly ground black pepper

1. Turn the yoghurt into a small, non-stick saucepan.
2. Juice the orange segments with the parsley and basil or celery.
3. Season lightly then stir, gradually, into the yoghurt.
4. Heat the sauce gently, stirring, and do not allow it to boil.
5. Serve the sauce immediately.

This recipe makes approximately 275ml (9fl oz) sauce.

Carrot and Tomato Sauce

This savoury sauce is delicious served with the Cheesy Nut and Vegetable Roast (see p. 197). Try it with freshly cooked pasta, topped with a sprinkling of grated cheese and chopped basil. It can also be served as a soup for two people.

Serves 4

3 tomatoes, sliced to fit juicer
½ medium onion, sliced to fit juicer
3 medium carrots, sliced to fit juicer
1 slice peeled lemon
A little sea salt and freshly ground black pepper
15ml (1 tablespoon) arrowroot
5ml (1 teaspoon) clear honey

1. Juice the tomatoes, onion, carrots and lemon. Season lightly.
2. Turn the juice into a medium size non-stick pan.
3. Blend the arrowroot with a little water, then stir this into the pan.
4. Bring to the boil, stirring, then simmer for 1–2 minutes. Stir in the honey and serve immediately.

This recipe makes approximately 400ml (14fl oz) sauce.

Onion and Sweet Pepper Sauce

A well flavoured and nutritious vegetable sauce. Green and red peppers contain lots of vitamin C and some A, B3 and B6. Serve this sauce with pasta, on vegetables and with fish dishes.

Serves 4

1 medium onion
1 red pepper
½ green pepper
1 courgette
A little sea salt and freshly ground black pepper
10ml (2 teaspoons) cornflour

1. Cut the onion, the red and green pepper and the courgette into juiceable pieces and place in a mixing bowl for easy handling.
2. With the motor running, juice the onion, peppers and courgette. Pour the juice into a medium saucepan and season lightly.
3. Blend the cornflour to a smooth paste with a little water then stir this into the juice.
4. Bring to the boil, stirring. Simmer for 1–2 minutes, then serve immediately.

This recipe makes approximately 350ml (12fl oz) sauce.

Orange and Lemon Sauce

A tangy, refreshing sauce that is delicious with roast duck and chicken. Try it also on ice cream or with pancakes.

Serves 4

3 large oranges
½ lemon
10ml (2 teaspoons) clear honey, or to taste
10ml (2 teaspoons) arrowroot

1. Peel the oranges and the lemon, removing half the pith and discarding the pips. Divide into juiceable slices and place in a bowl beside the juicing machine.
2. With the motor running, juice the oranges and lemon. Put the juice into a medium saucepan and add the honey.
3. Blend the arrowroot with a little water and stir this into the pan.
4. Bring to the boil, stirring, then simmer for 1–2 minutes. Serve immediately.

This recipe makes approximately 300ml (½ pint) sauce.

Salmon with Strawberry Sauce

An attractive dinner-party dish that's full of protein and vitamin C. It is quick to prepare and cook too. Serve with new potatoes and asparagus.

Serves 4

4 salmon steaks
15ml (1 tablespoon) olive oil
30ml (2 tablespoons) freshly chopped mixed herbs: parsley, thyme, basil, rosemary
A little sea salt and freshly ground black pepper

For the sauce
450g (1lb) fresh strawberries, cut to fit juicer
2 sprigs fresh mint
150ml (5fl oz) medium dry white wine
15ml (1 tablespoon) arrowroot
25g (1oz) caster sugar

To garnish
fresh strawberries
sprigs of watercress

1. Arrange the salmon steaks on a grill rack.
2. Put the oil into a small bowl. Add the herbs and a little seasoning. Mix well then spoon evenly over the fish.
3. Grill the salmon under a pre-heated medium grill for 8–10 minutes, until cooked, turning once.
4. Remove from heat and set aside to cool.
5. Meanwhile, prepare the sauce.
6. Juice the strawberries with the mint, on the juicer.
7. Put the juice into a medium size saucepan with the wine. Blend the arrowroot to a smooth paste with a little water and stir into the pan.
8. Heat the sauce, stirring continuously, until boiled and slightly thickened. Stir in the sugar, to dissolve.
9. Set aside until almost cold.
10. To serve, arrange a pool of strawberry sauce on four dinner plates. Top with a salmon steak and serve

immediately with the new potatoes and asparagus, garnished with the fresh strawberries and watercress.

Pasta with Sauce Provencale

A filling supper or lunch dish that's ideal for vegetarians. The juice gives the sauce an instant Mediterranean flavour.

Serves 4

For the Provencale sauce
2 sprigs fresh parsley
4 tomatoes, sliced to fit juicer
½ stick celery, cut to fit juicer
2 cloves garlic
½ medium onion, sliced to fit juicer
1 green pepper, de-seeded and sliced to fit juicer
30ml (2 tablespoons) tomato purée
90ml (6 tablespoons) red wine
10ml (2 teaspoons) dried oregano

30ml (2 tablespoons) corn oil
1 medium aubergine, diced
1 medium cauliflower, divided into florets
15ml (1 tablespoon) cornflour
A little sea salt and freshly ground black pepper

350g (12oz) spaghetti

1. Prepare the sauce by juicing the parsley with the tomatoes, celery, garlic, onion and green pepper.
2. Blend the tomato purée with the wine, then stir it into the juice with the oregano. Set aside.
3. Heat the oil in a large saucepan, add the aubergine and cauliflower and sauté for approximately 5 minutes, until the aubergine softens slightly.
4. Blend the cornflour with a little of the juice, then stir in the remaining juice. Season lightly. Add to the vegetables in the pan.
5. Bring to the boil, stirring, then cover and simmer for 8–10 minutes, until the vegetables are tender but firm.
6. Meanwhile, cook the spaghetti in a large pan of boiling water with 5ml (1 teaspoon) corn oil, until tender (8–10 minutes).

7. Drain the spaghetti and serve immediately, topped with the Provencale sauce.

Baked Mackerel in Vegetable Juice and Cider Sauce

Ready filleted mackerel, now available at many super-markets, are ideal for this recipe. The juice is mixed with cider to produce a delicious sauce.

Serves 4

4 large mackerel fillets
15ml (1 tablespoon) olive oil
1 medium onion, peeled and thinly sliced
2 medium size tomatoes
4 broccoli florets
½ handful fresh parsley
Cider (see method)
A little sea salt and freshly ground pepper
5ml (1 teaspoon) arrowroot

To serve
freshly chopped parsley

1. Pre-heat the oven to gas mark 4, 350°F (180°C).
2. Lay the mackerel, in a single layer, in a shallow oven proof dish.
3. Heat the oil in a small saucepan. Add the onion and sauté for 3–4 minutes. Turn the onions on to the mackerel.
4. Meanwhile, cut the tomatoes and broccoli to fit the juicer, then juice them with the parsley sprigs.
5. Pour the juice into a measuring jug and make it up to 225ml (8fl oz) with the cider.
6. Season liquid lightly and pour over the onions and fish.
7. Cover with a lid or foil and bake in the oven for 20 minutes.
8. Lift the mackerel on to a serving dish, set aside and keep warm.
9. Blend the arrowroot with a little water, then stir it into fish juices in the dish. Turn the sauce into a small pan.
10. Bring to the boil, stirring, then simmer for 1–2 minutes.
11. Pour the sauce over the mackerel and serve immediately, sprinkled with the chopped parsley.

Marinated Fruity Pork

A marinade is a mixture of oil with vinegar, wine or citrus juice and herbs used to soak poultry, meat or fish, before cooking, to make it more tender. This recipe has a Chinese flavour so serve the pork with rice or noodles and a green salad.

Serves 4

30ml (2 tablespoons) sunflower oil
A little sea salt and freshly ground black pepper
½ orange, peeled and cut into slices to fit juicer, discarding pips
1 stick celery, cut into pieces to fit juicer
¼ medium onion, sliced to fit juicer
¼ red pepper, de-seeded and sliced to fit juicer
½ handful mixed garden herbs
15ml (1 tablespoon) soy sauce
4 lean pork chops

1. Put the oil into a mug. Season with a little salt and freshly ground black pepper.
2. Using the juicer, juice the orange, celery, onion and red pepper, with the herbs.
3. Add the juice to the oil in the mug. Whisk lightly with a fork, adding the soy sauce.
4. Arrange the pork chops in a shallow dish.
6. Pour over the marinade. Cover and refrigerate for 2–4 hours, or overnight, turning the pork in the marinade once or twice.
7. Lift the chops from the marinade and cook under a pre-heated grill, turning occasionally, until well browned and cooked right through (about 20 minutes).
8. Serve immediately.

Marinated Chinese Chicken

Chicken breasts marinated in a piquant sauce, then baked in the oven, are simply delicious. Chicken is healthy food, particularly if the skin, which harbours most of the fat, is removed.

Serve with boiled rice and a mixed salad.

Serves 4

For the marinade
1 clove garlic
1 orange, peeled and cut into slices to fit juicer, discarding pips
1 medium size tomato, sliced to fit juicer
½ handful fresh parsley
15ml (1 tablespoon) soy sauce
15ml (1 tablespoon) tomato purée
15ml (1 tablespoon) sunflower oil

4 part-boned chicken breasts, skinned

1. Make the marinade. Juice the garlic, orange, tomato and parsley, then blend the juice with the soy sauce, tomato purée and sunflower oil.
2. Put the chicken, in a single layer, into a shallow dish. Pour the marinade over it and set aside, covered, for 2 hours, or overnight, turning the chicken in the marinade, once or twice.
3. Pre-heat the oven to gas mark 5, 375°F (190°C).
4. Lift the chicken pieces from the marinade and arrange in a roasting dish. Roast for approximately 45 minutes, basting occasionally, until the juices run clear when the meat is pierced with a sharp knife.
5. Serve immediately on a bed of rice, accompanied by a mixed salad.

Salads, Snacks
and Main Meals

Nothing beats home made dishes and, thanks to the quick and easy recipes in this section, cooking doesn't seem to be such a chore. With a juicer and a good supply of well washed fruit and vegetables, you are well on the way to producing a host of dishes that are both healthy and delicious.

Salads and vegetable dishes will be enhanced by these tasty dressings that are bursting with goodness. Next time you have friends round for drinks, serve Cheesy Tomato Dip (see p. 137) with vegetable sticks, which looks very pretty and colourful. Follow this with some of the main meal dishes such as the Juicy Beef Burgers (see p. 156) that are delicious cooked on the barbecue or grilled conventionally. The Mushroom Risotto (see p. 158) is ideal for vegetarians and for anyone trying to cut down their meat consumption.

Cheesy Tomato Dip

A creamy dip that's delicious served with vegetable sticks and fruits such as strawberries, cherries and grapes. Good on the buffet table or served with pre-dinner juices.

Serves 4

2 medium size tomatoes, sliced to fit juicer
1 wedge lemon, peeled and sliced to fit juicer, discarding pips
225g (8oz) medium fat soft cheese, such as curd or reduced-
    fat cream cheese
½ handful fresh basil, chopped
10ml (2 teaspoons) tomato purée

To serve
vegetable sticks and fresh fruits

1. Juice the tomatoes and lemon.
2. Turn the soft cheese into a mixing bowl. Gradually beat in the juice until combined. Beat in the basil and tomato purée.
3. Alternatively, put the cheese into a food processor; add the juice and process to mix evenly using the metal blade. Add the basil and tomato purée and process again for a few seconds.
4. Spoon the mixture into a serving dish and serve with the vegetable sticks and fresh fruits.

Tomato Sorbet

This delicious savoury ice is ideal served between courses to refresh the palate. Good too as a light first course to a dinner party. Slimmers will appreciate this full flavoured tomato ice.

Serves 2

1 lemon, peeled and sliced to fit juicer
750g (1½lb) tomatoes, sliced to fit juicer
½ small onion, sliced to fit juicer
1 handful fresh basil
15ml (1 tablespoon) tomato purée
5ml (1 teaspoon) clear honey

To serve
sliced cucumber

1. Place lemon, tomatoes, onion and basil into a large bowl beside the juicer, then juice them.
2. Blend the tomato purée and honey into the juice. Pour into a fairly shallow plastic container and freeze until the mixture just begins to get icy around the edges (about 1–1½ hours).
3. Turn into a chilled bowl and beat using a hand-held electric whisk.
4. Return to shallow container and freeze until solid.
5. Serve scoops of the sorbet, garnished with slices of cucumber.

Chinese Dressing

This simple dressing gives any salad an authentic oriental flavour. Ideal on green salads or a tomato salad.

Serves 4 to 6

½ lime
1 apple
½ handful fresh dill
5ml (1 teaspoon) light soy sauce
30ml (2 tablespoons) corn oil
Freshly ground black pepper

1. Using a zester, remove the rind from the lime and keep. Then peel the lime and cut into slices to fit the juicer, discarding the pips. Store in a bowl beside the juicer.
2. Slice the apple into juiceable pieces and put into the bowl with the lime and the dill.
3. With the motor running, juice the lime with the apple and dill.
4. Add the reserved peel to the juice with the soy sauce and the oil, and season with a little black pepper. Whisk lightly with a fork before using.

This recipe makes approximately 120ml (4fl oz) dressing.

Herby Salad Vinaigrette

A light vinaigrette made from grapes and herbs that's particularly suitable for any salad containing fruits.

Serves 4

100g (4oz) black or red grapes
½ handful fresh parsley
3 leaves lemon balm
45ml (3 tablespoons) olive oil
A little sea salt and finely ground black pepper

1. Discard any hard brown stems on the grapes, then juice them on the juicer, with the parsley and the lemon balm.
2. Add the oil to the juice with a little seasoning.
3. Whisk lightly with a fork before using.

This recipe makes approximately 200ml (7fl oz) vinaigrette.

Spiced Yoghurt Dressing

A low fat creamy dressing that's ideal for rice and pasta salads. Good too on new potatoes and celery.

Serves 4

1 medium size tomato, sliced to fit juicer
15ml (1 tablespoon) fresh coriander
1 apple, sliced to fit juicer
150ml (5fl oz) fromage frais or natural yoghurt
A little sea salt and freshly ground black pepper

1. With the motor running, juice the tomato with the coriander and apple.
2. Put the fromage frais into a mixing bowl and gradually stir in the juice.
3. Season to taste and serve immediately.

This recipe makes approximately 175ml (6fl oz) dressing.

Creamy Strawberry Dressing
with Herbs

A summery dressing that is good on pasta salads or with cold meat or fish dishes. Low in fat and high on taste with plenty of vitamin C.

Serves 4

225g (8oz) fresh strawberries, sliced to fit juicer
3 sprigs fresh mint
1 slice lemon
150ml (5fl oz) fromage frais
5ml (1 teaspoon) clear honey
A little sea salt and freshly ground black pepper

1. With the motor running, juice the strawberries with the mint and the lemon.
2. Turn the fromage frais into a mixing bowl and gradually stir in the juice and the honey.
3. Season to taste and use immediately.

This recipe makes approximately 250ml (8fl oz) dressing.

Carrot and Basil Dressing

Carrots give a pleasant, slightly sweet flavour to this unusual dressing which is delicious on mixed salads. Everyone will love the fresh taste.

Serves 4

4 medium size carrots, cut to fit juicer
2 medium size tomatoes, sliced to fit juicer
½ handful fresh basil
30ml (2 tablespoons) olive oil
A little freshly ground black pepper

1. Juice the carrots with the tomatoes and basil.
2. Add the oil to the juice and whisk lightly with a fork.
3. Season to taste and use immediately.

This recipe makes approximately 200ml (7fl oz) dressing.

Tomato, Celery and Chive Dressing

A fat-free dressing that is delicious on any salad that uses pulse vegetables. Fresh and lightly onion flavoured, it's also good on fennel and black grape salad.

Serves 4

4 large tomatoes, sliced to fit juicer
3 large sticks celery, cut to fit juicer
1 clove garlic
30ml (2 tablespoons) fresh chives
1 medium size carrot, cut to fit juicer
A little freshly ground black pepper

1. Juice the tomatoes on the juicer with the celery, garlic, chives and carrot.
2. Season the juice with the black pepper to taste, and use immediately.

This recipe makes approximately 175ml (6fl oz) dressing.

Orange and Lime Dressing

Use this tangy and refreshing dressing all year round on mixed salads or on almost any salad served with poultry. It's good too on coleslaw.

Serves 4

1 large orange, peeled and sliced to fit juicer, discarding pips
½ lime, peeled and sliced to fit juicer, discarding pips
½ handful fresh chervil or parsley
45ml (3 tablespoons) olive oil
A little sea salt and freshly ground black pepper

1. Juice the orange on the juicer with the lime and chervil or parsley.
2. Add the oil to the juice and whisk lightly with a fork.
3. Season to taste and use immediately.

This recipe makes approximately 175ml (6fl oz) dressing.

Fruity Curried Dressing

This wonderfully creamy dressing, flavoured with herbs, is a must for coleslaw. Make your coleslaw from a mixture of red and green cabbage with carrot and sultanas and add the dressing 20 minutes before serving to allow the flavours to mingle.

Serves 4 to 6

1 mango, cut into slices to fit juicer, discarding stone
1 5cm (2in) piece cucumber
4 sprigs fresh coriander
150ml (5fl oz) fromage frais
5ml (1 teaspoon) curry powder

1. Juice the mango on the juicer with the cucumber and coriander.
2. Turn the fromage frais into a mixing bowl.
3. Blend in the juice gradually, then add the curry powder. Use immediately.

This recipe makes approximately 200ml (7fl oz) dressing.

Green Salad with Lemon and Chive Dressing

This healthy salad is quick to assemble and looks attractive. Serve it with roast poultry as a change from hot vegetables or with quiche or cold meats.

Serves 4 to 6

For the dressing
1 wedge lemon, peeled and sliced to fit juicer, discarding pips
1 stick celery, cut into pieces
1 medium size tomato, sliced to fit juicer
½ handful fresh parsley
30ml (2 tablespoons) olive oil
Freshly ground black pepper

For the salad
1 Cos lettuce
1 large bulb fennel
1 green pepper, de-seeded
1 carton mustard and cress

1. Make the dressing by juicing the lemon with the celery, tomato and parsley. Whisk in the olive oil and freshly ground black pepper, lightly, with a fork. Set aside.
2. Tear the lettuce roughly with your hands and put into a salad bowl. Slice the fennel and the green pepper finely, either by hand, or using the slicing disc on the food processor. Add to the bowl.
3. Using scissors, snip the mustard and cress into the bowl.
4. Just before serving, pour dressing on to salad and toss to coat. Serve immediately.

Mixed Salad with Grapefruit Dressing

This colourful, crisp salad uses few ingredients so is quick to assemble and the grapefruit dressing is wonderfully tangy and refreshing. Serve with beefburgers and other minced beef recipes such as spaghetti Bolognese, lasagne, etc.

Serves 4 to 6

For the dressing
¼ pink grapefruit, peeled and sliced to fit juicer, discarding pips
4 sprigs fresh parsley
1 clove garlic
¼ onion, sliced to fit juicer
85ml (3fl oz) olive oil
A little sea salt and freshly ground black pepper
2.5ml (½ teaspoon) soft brown sugar
2.5ml (½ teaspoon) dried mustard powder

For the salad
½ Iceberg lettuce
1 Little Gem lettuce
2 sticks celery, chopped
1 courgette, sliced
1 red apple

1. Prepare the dressing. Assemble the grapefruit with the parsley, garlic and onion in a bowl beside the juicer.
2. With the motor running, juice the ingredients.
3. Whisk the olive oil into the juice, using a fork, with seasoning to taste. Add the sugar and mustard powder and set aside.
4. Prepare the salad. Shred the lettuce into a salad bowl. Add the celery and courgette and lastly core and chop the apple and add it to the bowl.
5. Whisk the dressing again, then pour it on to the salad.
6. Toss ingredients together and serve immediately.

Brown Rice Salad with Grape and Kiwi Dressing

A useful salad that contains plenty of energy-giving carbo-hydrate with fibre and vitamins. Serve with a leaf salad and meat, fish or vegetarian dishes.

Serves 4

225g (8oz) brown rice, cooked and cooled
½ red pepper, de-seeded and chopped
1 courgette, finely sliced
2 spring onions, chopped
75g (3oz) roasted peanuts

For the dressing
100g (4oz) black grapes, dark brown stems removed
1 kiwi fruit, sliced to fit juicer
½ handful fresh parsley
45ml (3 tablespoons) corn oil
Pinch of curry powder

1. Put the rice into a large mixing bowl. Add the red pepper with the courgette, onions and peanuts.
2. Prepare the dressing. Juice the black grapes on the juicer with the kiwi fruit and the parsley. Add the oil to the juice with the curry powder. Whisk lightly with a fork.
3. Pour the dressing over the salad ingredients and toss lightly until well mixed.
4. Serve immediately.

Garden Salad

A combination of colourful raw ingredients with a deliciously fruity dressing. A healthy base to any meal, it is ideal served with fish, chicken or cottage cheese.

Serves 4

225g (8oz) red cabbage
225g (8oz) Chinese leaves
2 medium size tomatoes
6 button mushrooms
3 spring onions
½ red pepper, de-seeded and cut into 3 pieces

For the dressing
1 orange
½ handful fresh parsley
1 clove garlic, crushed
45ml (3 tablespoons) olive oil
Freshly ground black pepper

1. Using the slicing disc on a food processor, shred the red cabbage and transfer it to a large salad bowl. Using the same disc, shred the Chinese leaves. Add these to the bowl.
2. Slice the tomatoes by hand and add to the bowl.
3. With the metal blade, roughly chop the mushrooms, spring onions and red pepper. Add to the bowl.
4. Prepare the dressing. Grate the rind from the orange then peel, segment and juice it on the juicer. Add the reserved orange rind with the chopped parsley, garlic, oil and black pepper. Whisk lightly with a fork. Turn dressing on to the salad.
5. Toss all the ingredients, then serve immediately.

Red Kidney Bean and Celery Salad

This colourful salad is full of fibre and vitamins with plenty of body building protein. Serve it with other salads on the buffet table; it's ideal for special occasions.

Serves 4

For the dressing
1 mango, peeled and sliced to fit juicer, discarding central
    stone
½ lime, peeled and sliced to fit juicer, discarding pips
2 sprigs fresh rosemary
30ml (2 tablespoons) olive oil
Freshly ground black pepper

For the salad
1 430g (15oz) can red kidney beans, drained and rinsed
3 large sticks celery, chopped fairly finely
2 spring onions, finely chopped
2 hard boiled eggs, chopped
15ml (1 tablespoon) freshly chopped parsley

1. Make the dressing. Juice the mango with the lime and rosemary. Whisk the olive oil into the juice with a little black pepper. Set aside.
2. Turn the red kidney beans into a large mixing bowl. Add the celery, onions, eggs and parsley. Toss lightly.
3. Just before serving, pour the dressing on to the salad ingredients. Toss again, just to coat.
4. Turn into a salad bowl and serve immediately.

Oriental Stir-Fry

Stir-frying is so quick and easy and with a juicer you can make a quick stir-fry sauce that is bursting with health. Family and friends are sure to be impressed with this oriental-style dish.

Serves 4

For the stir-fry sauce
3 medium size tomatoes
2 carrots
½ medium size red pepper
1 5cm (2in) piece cucumber
30ml (2 tablespoons) soy sauce
15ml (1 tablespoon) sherry
10ml (2 teaspoons) cornflour

For the stir-fry
30ml (2 tablespoons) sunflower oil
1 small onion, chopped
2 courgettes, sliced
2 sticks celery, chopped
100g (4oz) button mushrooms, sliced
2 carrots, cut into matchsticks
15ml (1 tablespoon) fresh coriander, chopped
8 crab sticks, chopped roughly
350g (12oz) peeled prawns, defrosted if frozen

1. Make the stir-fry sauce using the juicer. Cut the tomatoes, carrots, pepper and cucumber into pieces to fit the juicer. Store in a mixing bowl.
2. With the motor running, extract juice from sauce vegetables. Set aside.
3. Make the stir-fry. Heat the oil in a wok or large frying pan. Stir-fry the onion for 2–3 minutes, until softened, then add the courgettes, celery, mushrooms and carrots. Stir-fry for 4 minutes.
4. Add the soy sauce and sherry to the stir-fry sauce, then blend in the cornflour. Pour this sauce into the wok or frying pan. Add the coriander. Bring to the boil, stirring. Simmer for 2 minutes. Add the crab sticks and prawns to

the stir-fry and heat through. Serve immediately with rice or noodles.

Turkey Stir-Fry

A healthy recipe that's quick to prepare and cook. Serve with brown rice or wholegrain noodles. A mixed salad would complement the meal well.

Serves 4

For the sauce
1 5cm (2in) slice fresh pineapple, cut into strips to fit juicer
1 large orange, peeled and sliced, discarding pips
½ handful fresh parsley
15ml (1 tablespoon) clear honey
30ml (2 tablespoons) soy sauce
10ml (2 teaspoons) arrowroot

For the stir-fry
30ml (2 tablespoons) corn oil
450g (1lb) turkey breast fillet, thinly sliced
1 bunch spring onions, chopped
2 sticks celery, chopped
1 red pepper, de-seeded and chopped
100g (4oz) bean sprouts

1. Juice the pineapple, orange and parsley. Set aside.
2. Heat the oil in a large frying pan or wok.
3. Stir-fry the turkey for 2–3 minutes.
4. Add the onions, celery and red pepper. Stir-fry for 3 minutes, then add the bean sprouts and stir-fry for a further 2 minutes.
5. Add the honey and soy sauce to the juice with the arrowroot. Stir to blend.
6. Pour the juice mixture into the stir-fry.
7. Bring to the boil, stirring continuously. Simmer for 1–2 minutes, stirring until sauce thickens slightly.
8. Serve immediately.

Pork in Plum Sauce

A deliciously different stir-fry recipe. The flavour of the plums is wonderful with pork. Serve with rice or noodles. Lemon balm is an aromatic herb with a pronounced flavour.

Serves 4

For the sauce
1 medium carrot, cut into pieces to fit juicer
1 large spring onion
4 plums, stoned and sliced to fit juicer
½ handful lemon balm
60ml (4 tablespoons) soy sauce
30ml (2 tablespoons) sherry

Garnish
30ml (2 tablespoons) pine nuts

For the stir-fry
30ml (2 tablespoons) corn oil
1 medium onion, peeled and chopped
450g (1lb) pork fillet, diced
1 green pepper, de-seeded and cut into strips
1 fresh ripe peach, peeled and diced, discarding stone

1. Make the sauce by juicing the carrot with the spring onion, plums and lemon balm. Stir the soy sauce and sherry into the juice and set aside.
2. In a clean, dry wok or large frying pan, dry fry the pine nuts until lightly toasted. Set aside.
3. Heat the oil in the pan, then add the onion and stir-fry for 2 minutes. Add the pork and stir-fry for 4–5 minutes. Add the green pepper and stir-fry for 2 minutes.
4. Add the peach and the sauce from the juicer and heat, stirring, for 3–4 minutes. Serve immediately, garnished with the pine nuts.

Juicy Beefburgers

A very simple way to make tasty, authentic burgers, using lean mince and all the goodness of juice. Serve with salad in large wholemeal rolls or granary baps and wait for friends to ask for the recipe!

Serves 4

450g (1lb) lean minced beef
2 slices wholemeal bread, crusts removed
A little sea salt and freshly ground black pepper
5ml (1 teaspoon) dry mustard powder

For the juice
1 stick celery, cut into pieces to fit juicer
1 medium size carrot, cut into pieces to fit juicer
½ onion, sliced to fit juicer
1 clove garlic
1 handful fresh herbs (mint, thyme, parsley, basil, rosemary)

To serve
mixed salad
wholemeal rolls or granary baps

1. Put the minced beef into a large mixing bowl.
2. Break the bread into pieces and make into breadcrumbs in a food processor, using the metal blade, or grate bread into crumbs. Add to the minced beef. Season lightly with the salt and pepper. Mix in the mustard powder.
3. Assemble all the ingredients to be juiced in a large mixing bowl, next to the juicer.
4. With the motor running, juice the celery with the carrot, onion, garlic and herbs.
5. Add juice to the meat and mix well until combined.
6. Form into four even-sized burgers.
7. Grill under a pre-heated medium grill for 10–15 minutes, turning once or twice, until cooked.
8. Serve in a split bap or roll, accompanied by the mixed salad.

Fruity Pork Burgers

Apple juice with tomatoes and herbs enhances the sweet flavour of lean pork in these 'moreish' burgers. Serve in large bap rolls with tomato relish for a tasty quick lunch or supper. A green salad would also go well with the burgers.

Serves 4

450g (1lb) lean minced pork
2 slices wholemeal bread, crusts removed
A little sea salt and freshly ground black pepper

For the juice
1 apple, sliced to fit juicer
1 tomato, sliced to fit juicer
2 spring onions, sliced to fit juicer
1 clove garlic
1 handful fresh parsley

To serve
bap rolls
tomato relish

1. Put the minced pork into a large mixing bowl.
2. Break the bread into pieces and make into breadcrumbs in a food processor, using the metal blade, or grate bread into crumbs. Add to the minced pork and season lightly.
3. Assemble all the ingredients to be juiced in a bowl next to the juicer.
4. With the motor running, juice the apple with the tomato, spring onions, garlic and parsley.
5. Add juice to the meat and mix well until combined.
6. Form into four even-sized burgers.
7. Grill under a pre-heated medium grill for 10–15 minutes, turning once or twice, until well cooked and golden brown.
8. Serve in the split baps with some tomato relish.

Mushroom Risotto

Quick to prepare and make, this well-flavoured risotto makes a quick vegetarian supper dish. Serve with a mixed salad and French or garlic bread.

Serves 4

2 medium size tomatoes, sliced to fit juicer
1 handful fresh parsley
1 medium onion, sliced to fit juicer
1 stick celery, chopped to fit juicer
1 carrot, chopped to fit juicer
30ml (2 tablespoons) corn oil
1 clove garlic, chopped
225g (8oz) button mushrooms, sliced
225g (8oz) brown rice
100g (4oz) dried apricots, chopped
1 courgette, thinly sliced
225g (8oz) bean sprouts

To serve
45ml (3 tablespoons) Parmesan cheese
25g (1oz) toasted pine nuts

1. Assemble the tomatoes, parsley, onion, celery and carrot in a bowl near the juicing machine, then juice them. Pour into a measuring jug and make up to 600ml (1 pint) with water.
2. Heat the oil in a medium size, heavy-based pan, and fry the garlic and mushrooms for about 3 minutes. Add the rice and stir to coat with oil.
3. Add the apricots with the liquid from the juicer.
4. Bring to the boil, then cover and simmer for 30 minutes. Add the courgette with the bean sprouts and continue to cook, covered, for 5 minutes, until the rice is tender.
5. Serve immediately, sprinkled with the Parmesan cheese and pine nuts.

Speedy Beef Casserole

When you haven't the time for chopping and peeling, turn to the juicer for a delicious casserole. Adding a few frozen vegetables towards the end of cooking gives the casserole quick texture and colour.

Serves 4

4 tomatoes, sliced to fit juicer
½ medium onion, sliced to fit juicer
1 courgette, sliced to fit juicer
½ orange, peeled and sliced to fit juicer, discarding pips
3 carrots, cut to fit juicer
1 red pepper, cut to fit juicer
1 green pepper, cut to fit juicer
450g (1lb) lean casserole beef, cubed
30ml (2 tablespoons) wholemeal flour
30ml (2 tablespoons) olive oil
A little sea salt and freshly ground black pepper
225g (8oz) frozen mixed vegetables (peas, carrots, cauliflower)

To serve
freshly chopped basil

1. Assemble the prepared tomatoes, onion, courgette, orange, carrots and the red and green peppers in a bowl beside the juicer. Juice them and set aside.
2. Toss the beef in the flour to coat evenly.
3. Heat the oil in a large casserole dish then add the beef, in small batches, and fry until evenly browned on all sides.
4. Stir the juice from the juicer into the beef. Season lightly with the salt and pepper.
5. Cover with a lid and simmer for 1½ hours, until the beef is tender.
6. Stir the frozen vegetables into the casserole and continue to simmer for 5–7 minutes.
7. Serve immediately, sprinkled with the chopped basil.

Apricot and Watercress Stuffing

A fruity stuffing that's wonderful in chicken and also good with pork or duck. This recipe is sufficient to stuff a 1.4kg (3lb) bird and is quick and easy to prepare.

2 spring onions, chopped to fit juicer
1 stick celery, cut to fit juicer
2 apricots, sliced to fit juicer, discarding stone
75g (3oz) brown rice, cooked and cooled
1 small bunch watercress, de-stalked and chopped
A little sea salt and freshly ground black pepper

1. Assemble the spring onions with the celery and apricots in a bowl near the juicing machine, then juice them.
2. Put the rice and the watercress into a large mixing bowl. Add the juice from the machine. Mix well, seasoning with a little salt and pepper.
3. Use as required.

Tomato and Olive Oil Bread

This healthy bread is quick to make as there's no yeast involved. The tomato juice gives a wonderful flavour to the loaf, which is delicious served freshly baked with cheese and relish, or toasted with scrambled eggs. Either way you'll be impressed with the true tomato flavour. You will need a 450g (1lb) loaf tin.

Makes: 1 450g (1lb) loaf

400g (14oz) self-raising wholemeal flour
30ml (2 tablespoons) fresh garden herbs (parsley, basil, thyme, rosemary)
1 clove garlic
225g (8oz) tomatoes, cut to fit juicer
45ml (3 tablespoons) olive oil
2 eggs, size 3
A little sea salt and freshly ground black pepper
25g (1oz) reduced fat Cheddar cheese, grated

1. Pre-heat the oven to gas mark 5, 375°F (190°C).
2. Lightly grease the loaf tin.
3. Put the flour into a mixing bowl.
4. With the motor running, juice the herbs with the garlic and the tomatoes. Transfer the juice to a measuring jug and make it up to 250ml (8fl oz) with water.
5. Stir the oil into the flour. Beat the eggs together, then add them to the flour mixture with the tomato juice.
6. Season lightly, then mix well. Turn into the prepared tin.
7. Top evenly with the grated cheese.
8. Stand tin on a baking sheet and bake the loaf, near the top of the oven, for approximately 55 minutes.
9. Turn on to a wire rack to cool.
10. Serve sliced, spread with polyunsaturated margarine or low fat spread.

Desserts

Speedy delicious milk shakes with plenty of protein and calcium; delicate sorbets that are excellent for cleansing the palate; jellies with the full flavour of fresh fruits – there are recipes for all these in this section. Try Grape Ice Cream (see p. 175) or Fruits of the Forest Sorbet (see p. 167). Make both for a choice of standby desserts in the freezer that everyone will love. Remember it's a good idea to remove all home made ice creams and sorbets from the freezer and store them in the fridge for 45 minutes before serving.

Peach and Nectarine Shake

Fresh fruit mixed with cold milk and ice cream makes a delicious drink with plenty of protein, calcium and vitamins.

Serves 2

2 peaches, sliced to fit juicer, discarding central stone
1 ripe nectarine, sliced to fit juicer, discarding central stone
350ml (12fl oz) ice cold semi-skimmed milk
2 scoops vanilla ice cream

1. With the motor running, juice the peaches and the nectarine.
2. Put the juice, milk and ice cream into a food processor, using the metal blade, and process to mix well.
3. Serve immediately in tall tumblers.

This recipe makes approximately 475ml (16fl oz) shake.

Kiwi Shake with Strawberries

A wonderfully foamy fruity shake that tastes clean and refreshing. Serve ice cold with big straws and a slice of lime on the edge of the glass.

Serves 2

2 kiwi fruit, sliced to fit juicer
10 strawberries, sliced to fit juicer
350ml (12fl oz) semi-skimmed milk
2 scoops vanilla ice cream

To serve
slices of lime

1. Juice the kiwi fruit and the strawberries.
2. Put the juice into a food processor, using the metal blade.
3. Add the milk with the ice cream and process until combined.
4. Divide between two tumblers, decorate with the lime, and serve immediately.

This recipe makes approximately 475ml (16fl oz) shake.

Fruits of the Forest Sorbet

This refreshing water-ice makes a delightful dessert, or serve it with Grape Ice Cream (see p. 175) for a real treat. Make plenty when soft fruits are cheap and abundant, as it will store in the freezer for up to three months.

Serves 4

225g (8oz) redcurrants or blackcurrants
450g (1lb) strawberries, halved if necessary
100g (4oz) raspberries
1 sprig fresh mint
caster sugar to taste
4 egg whites, size 2

1. Assemble the currants, the strawberries and the raspberries with the mint in a bowl beside the juicer, then juice them.
2. Turn the juice into a large mixing bowl. Stir in sugar to taste.
3. Pour into a rigid container, cover, and freeze until mushy (about 1½ hours).
4. Beat the egg whites until they stand in soft peaks, then turn the semi-frozen sorbet into a large mixing bowl and blend in the egg whites quickly and evenly using an electric whisk.
5. Return the sorbet to the freezer and leave to freeze solid.

Bananas in Black Grape Jelly

This refreshing and well-flavoured jelly is popular at dinner parties. The mint is delicious with the fruit. Serve with Greek yoghurt or a little single cream.

Serves 4 to 6

15g (1 0.4oz sachet plus 5ml (1 teaspoon)) powdered gelatine
225g (8oz) black grapes, brown stems discarded
2 Granny Smith apples, sliced to fit juicer
2 medium bananas

1. Sprinkle gelatine over 60ml (4 tablespoons) water in a small bowl. Leave for 10 minutes, then dissolve over a pan of hot water, stirring continuously. Set aside.
2. Assemble the grapes and apples in a bowl beside the juicing machine, then juice them.
3. Pass the juice through a sieve into a measuring jug and make it up to 450ml (15fl oz) with water if necessary. Stir the dissolved gelatine into the fruit juice.
4. Peel and slice the bananas into an attractive glass serving dish and pour over the jelly mixture.
5. Refrigerate overnight to set.

Pears in Real Orange Jelly

This real fruit jelly is a low calorie dessert that's popular with children and adults alike. Serve with ice cream or yoghurt.

Serves 4 to 6

15g (1 0.4oz sachet plus 5ml (1 teaspoon)) powdered gelatine
3 large oranges, peeled and sliced to fit juicer, discarding pips
100g (4oz) white grapes, brown stems discarded
3 pears

1. Sprinkle gelatine over 60ml (4 tablespoons) water in a small bowl. Leave for 10 minutes, then dissolve over a pan of hot water, stirring continuously. Set aside.
2. Assemble the oranges and grapes in a bowl beside the juicing machine, then juice them.
3. Measure the juice and make it up to 450ml (15fl oz) with water. Stir the dissolved gelatine into the fruit juice.
4. Peel, core and slice the pears into an attractive glass serving dish. Pour over the jelly mixture.
5. Refrigerate overnight to set.

Green Fruit Salad in Grape Juice

Making a fruit salad entirely from green fruits is surprisingly pleasing to the eye, and will refresh palates after any meal. It's also a low fat dessert if served with natural yoghurt, a little single cream or fromage frais.

Serves 4

For the juice base
225g (8oz) green grapes, brown stems discarded
½ lime, peeled and cut to fit juicer, discarding pips

For the fruit salad
1 canteloupe melon
1 kiwi fruit, peeled and sliced
225g (8oz) green grapes
1 green apple, cored and chopped
30ml (2 tablespoons) Midori melon liqueur or creme de menthe (optional)

1. For the fruit juice base, juice the grapes in the juicer with the lime. Pour into a large mixing bowl.
2. Either ball or dice the melon flesh and add to the bowl with the kiwi fruit, grapes and apple.
3. Add the liqueur, if using. Toss everything together lightly and serve immediately.

Raspberry Fool with Bananas

This tangy fruit fool uses some whipping cream with low fat fromage frais to produce a delicious dessert that tastes as though it was made with double cream. A very pretty dessert; serve it in wine glasses or sundae dishes.

Serves 4

150ml (5fl oz) whipping cream
85ml (3fl oz) low fat fromage frais
50g (2oz) caster sugar
225g (8oz) fresh raspberries
1 slice peeled lemon
2 bananas, sliced

To serve
sprigs of fresh mint

1. Put the cream into a large mixing bowl and whip, using an electric whisk, until standing in soft peaks.
2. Fold the fromage frais into the whipped cream with the caster sugar.
3. Juice the raspberries in the juicer with the slice of lemon.
4. Gradually fold the juice into the cream mixture, until combined. Fold in the bananas.
5. Turn into four sundae dishes and serve immediately, decorated with the sprigs of mint.

Peach Fool with Toasted Almonds

A speedy, light dessert that appeals equally to children and to adults. Serve with almond wafers for a dessert that is low in fat with plenty of calcium and flavour.

Serves 2

1 large peach, sliced to fit juicer, discarding stone
200g (7oz) Greek yoghurt or fromage frais
clear honey to taste

To serve
50g (2oz) toasted flaked almonds

1. Juice the peach on the machine.
2. Turn the yoghurt or fromage frais into a large mixing bowl and gradually blend in the peach juice. Add honey to taste.
3. Serve in individual sundae dishes, topped with the toasted almonds.

Fresh Fruit Salad

A colourful, healthy finale to any meal. The fruit juice base is quick and easy to prepare using the juicer. Serve with fromage frais or Greek yoghurt.

Serves 4

For the juice base
225g (8oz) green grapes, brown stems discarded
1 large orange, peeled and cut to fit juicer, discarding pips

For the fruit salad
2 oranges
1 red apple
1 green apple
1 kiwi fruit, peeled and sliced
1 large peach or nectarine, chopped, discarding stone

1. For the fruit juice base, juice the grapes with the orange in the juicer. Pour into a large mixing bowl.
2. Prepare the fruit salad. Hold the oranges over the bowl as you peel and segment them, discarding pith and peel, so that any juice will fall into it.
3. Core and chop the apples and add these to the bowl with the kiwi fruit.
4. Chop the peach or nectarine and add to the rest of the fruit.
5. Toss together lightly, so that the fruit is well coated with the juice, and serve immediately.

Real Fruity Ice Cream

The true flavour of the fruit comes through in this delicious ice cream. Greek yoghurt is used instead of double cream for a healthier dessert, but it does still contain animal fat.

Serves 4

225g (8oz) strawberries, cut to fit juicer
225g (8oz) blackcurrants
½ lemon, peeled and sliced, discarding pips
200g (7oz) Greek yoghurt
75g (3oz) caster sugar

To serve
fresh strawberries
fresh mint

1. With the motor running, juice the strawberries, black-currants and lemon.
2. Turn out the yoghurt into a large mixing bowl. Gradually blend in the fruit juice and the sugar.
3. Freeze until the mixture just begins to get icy around the edges (about 2 hours).
4. Turn into a chilled bowl and beat using a hand-held electric whisk.
5. Pour into a shallow container. Cover with a lid and freeze until solid.
6. Serve in sundae dishes, decorated with the fresh strawberries and sprigs of mint.

Grape Ice Cream

A superb sweet for a summer dinner party. Serve scoops of the ice cream in wine glasses, with crisp almond wafers. Add a scoop of Fruits of the Forest Sorbet (see p. 167) for an extra-special dessert.

Serves 6

425ml (¾ pint) double cream
300ml (½ pint) single cream
350g (12oz) green grapes, brown stems discarded
1 orange, peeled and segmented, discarding pips
75g (3oz) caster sugar
100g (4oz) macaroons, roughly crushed

To serve
fresh orange segments

1. Whisk the double and single cream together, using an electric mixer, until floppy.
2. With the machine running, extract juice from the grapes and orange.
3. Beat the fruit juice gradually into the whipped cream, then fold in the sugar.
4. Turn into a shallow, plastic container and leave in the freezer until the mixture begins to freeze around the edges (about 2 hours).
5. Turn into a chilled bowl and beat again, using a hand held electric mixer.
6. Fill the container with alternate layers of ice cream and crushed macaroons. Freeze for at least 2 hours.
7. To serve, arrange scoops of ice cream in wine glasses. Decorate with segments of fresh orange and serve immediately.

Plum Crumble

A crumble with a special fruity taste. This healthy dessert has plenty of fibre. Serve with custard made from semi-skimmed milk, or reduced fat ice cream.

Serves 4 to 6

2 large oranges, peeled and sliced to fit juicer, discarding pips
450g (1lb) plums, halved and stoned
1 medium size Cox's Orange Pippin apple, peeled, cored and
   sliced
50g (2oz) demerara sugar

For the topping
100g (4oz) rolled porridge oats
100g (4oz) plain wholemeal flour
100g (4oz) polyunsaturated margarine
75g (3oz) demerara sugar

1. Pre-heat the oven to gas mark 4, 350°F (180°C).
2. With the motor running, extract the juice from the oranges.
3. Put the prepared plums into a deep 1.2 litre (2 pint) pie dish with the apple. Pour the juice from the orange over the fruit. Add sugar and mix everything together.
4. Put oats and flour into a clean mixing bowl and rub in the margarine. Fork in the sugar evenly.
5. Spoon the topping evenly over the fruits.
6. Bake for 45–50 minutes, until golden.
7. Serve immediately with custard or ice cream.

Orange Gateau with Lemon Frosting

Serve small slices of this rather moreish cake. Although it looks wicked, it is made with polyunsaturated margarine, and topped with a low fat cheese mixture so it is healthier than many other cakes.

You will need 2 20cm (8in) non-stick sandwich tins, lightly greased and base lined.

Serves 8

For the cake
175g (6oz) polyunsaturated margarine, at room temperature
175g (6oz) caster sugar
175g (6oz) wholemeal self-raising flour (fine grade if possible)
3 eggs, size 2

For the filling
1 orange, peeled and sliced to fit juicer, discarding pips
30ml (2 tablespoons) Grand Marnier liqueur
150ml (5fl oz) double cream
2 large peaches, peeled and chopped, discarding stone

For the topping
175g (6oz) Philadelphia Light low fat soft cheese
10ml (2 teaspoons) lemon juice
75g (3oz) icing sugar, sieved

1. Make the cake. Pre-heat the oven to gas mark 4, 350°F (180°C).
2. Mix the cake by the one stage method. Put all the ingredients for the cake into a food processor and process using the metal blade. Gradually increase the speed, if the machine offers this facility, until well mixed. It will be necessary to stop the machine once or twice and scrape the mixture from the sides of the bowl into the centre with a spatula. Alternatively, put all the ingredients for the cake into a mixing bowl and mix with a wooden spoon to combine. Then beat for 2 minutes.
3. Divide the mixture evenly between the tins. Level the surface and bake for 25–30 minutes in the centre of the

177

oven, until lightly golden and springy to the touch. Turn out on to a wire cooling rack and allow to cool completely.

4. Meanwhile prepare the filling and topping. Juice the orange in the juicer then stir in the Grand Marnier. Pour into a small jug and set aside.

5. In a clean bowl, whip the cream until just stiff. Using the metal blade, purée the peaches in the food processor, then add the whipped cream and process just to blend. Set aside.

6. Prepare the topping. Put the low fat cheese into a large mixing bowl. Beat in the lemon juice with the icing sugar, until the mixture is light and fluffy. Alternatively, using the metal blade, put the cheese into the clean processor, add the lemon juice with the icing sugar and process until blended.

7. To assemble the gateau arrange one half of the sponge on a serving plate. Spoon or brush the orange juice and Grand Marnier mixture evenly over the surface.

8. Spread the peach and cream mixture all over the sponge layer. Top with the remaining sponge.

9. Spread lemon frosting evenly over the top of the cake. Swirl up with a knife and serve immediately.

Recipes for the Food Processor

The food processor makes an ideal partner to the juicer. This ingenious piece of equipment will blend cake mixes, batters etc., purée cooked fruits and vegetables, mince meat, chicken etc., chop, shred, grate, slice and whisk. It is quick, efficient, has a few simple to fit attachments, and is easy to wash up.

Whilst the juicer extracts all the vitamin and mineral rich juice from ingredients, leaving the fibre behind in the hopper, the food processor can purée certain ingredients in their entirety. It is therefore a useful addition to the kitchen and extremely valuable for the healthy eater who, for instance, can lightly cook vegetables in the minimum of water, then purée the whole contents of the pan and serve them as a delicious sauce.

A few hints

1. If the recipe requires the machine to be used for several processes, such as chopping vegetables, making a crumble topping and also a sauce, always start with the dry operation, progressing to the sauce, which should be processed last. This way you'll only have to wash the machine up once: at the end.
2. When using the machine to slice, place ingredients such as carrots and courgettes upright in the food chute, filling it completely to ensure perfectly shaped slices.
3. When grating, pack the food horizontally into the feed tube to produce long strips.
4. Slice cabbage for coleslaw using the slicing disc as the metal blade tends to overprocess cabbage, chopping it too finely.
5. Always arm yourself with a flexible spatula when you are processing sauces, making cake mixes, etc., as you will have to stop the machine and scrape ingredients from the side of the bowl to the centre, then process again for perfect results.
6. Don't overprocess, as you can turn minced meat, for instance, into a purée in seconds!

Avocado Dip

A creamy dip that's rich in vitamin D from the evaporated milk and vitamins A, B, C, D and E from the avocado. Calcium is present in both avocados and evaporated milk. Contains some fat. Avocados discolour rapidly so it's best to prepare this dip just before serving.

Serves 6

½ small onion, peeled and halved
2 large ripe avocados, peeled, stoned and roughly chopped
200ml (7fl oz) low fat evaporated milk
30ml (2 tablespoons) lime juice, from a fresh lime
30ml (2 tablespoons) fresh parsley
A little sea salt and freshly ground black pepper

To serve
vegetable sticks

1. Using the metal blade, process the onion until finely chopped.
2. Add the avocados to the food processor and blend until puréed.
3. Add the evaporated milk, lime juice, parsley and seasoning.
4. Blend until smooth.
5. Adjust the seasoning, then serve immediately with the vegetable sticks.

Carrot and Celery Dip

This subtly flavoured dip is low in calories, so slimmers can enjoy it. Serve with toast and vegetable sticks as an unusual starter or with pre-dinner drinks.

Serves 6

350g (12oz) carrots
3 sticks celery, chopped
150ml (5fl oz) vegetable stock
45ml (3 tablespoons) Greek yoghurt
15ml (1 tablespoon) fresh coriander
1 clove garlic, peeled and crushed
A little sea salt and freshly ground black pepper

To serve
toast and vegetable sticks

1. Slice the scrubbed carrots and celery in the food processor, using the slicing disc. Transfer to a medium saucepan.
2. Add the stock to the pan. Bring to the boil, then cover and simmer for 20 minutes, until vegetables are tender. Set aside to cool.
3. Turn contents of the pan into the food processor, using the metal blade. Add the yoghurt, coriander, garlic and a seasoning of salt and pepper.
4. Process to a smooth purée. Adjust the seasoning, then turn into a paté dish and refrigerate for at least an hour before serving.

Mayonnaise with Variations

Mayonnaise, made in the food processor, couldn't be easier or more delicious! Beware, even when made with poly-unsaturated oil this traditional salad dressing is laden with calories, so go easy on it. Try one of the delicious variations and experiment by thinning the mayonnaise with some fromage frais for a less fattening sauce.

Makes approximately 300ml (10fl oz) mayonnaise

1 egg yolk, size 3
1 egg, size 3
2.5ml (½ teaspoon) dry mustard powder
A little sea salt and freshly ground black pepper
300ml (½ pint) salad oil (sunflower, corn or olive)
15ml (1 tablespoon) white wine or cider vinegar

1. Using the metal blade, place egg yolk and egg, mustard and a little salt and freshly ground pepper into the food processor. Process for 5 seconds.
2. With the machine running, gradually add the oil, one drip at a time, using the drip feed in the 'pusher' if there is one. It may be added slightly more quickly once an emulsion forms (i.e. when the mayonnaise starts to thicken).
3. When all the oil has been incorporated into a thick mayonnaise, add the vinegar and process to combine.

Tomato and Parsley
Chop ½ handful parsley in the machine and stir into the mayonnaise with 10ml (2 teaspoons) tomato purée.

Garlic and Spring Onion
Chop 2 garlic cloves and 4 spring onions in the machine and stir into the mayonnaise.

Anchovy and Caper Paté

A deliciously different paté with a distinctively fishy taste. Serve with melba toast, carrot and celery sticks and a few radishes.

Serves 6

75g (3oz) crustless wholemeal bread
½ red pepper, de-seeded and cut into 4
1 50g (2oz) can anchovy fillets with capers, in oil
150ml (5fl oz) fromage frais
5ml (1 teaspoon) tomato purée
15ml (1 tablespoon) lemon juice
1 clove garlic, peeled and cut into 4
½ handful fresh parsley
Freshly ground black pepper

To serve
freshly made melba toast
carrot and celery sticks
radishes

1. Break the bread into pieces and put into the food processor. Using the metal blade, process into bread-crumbs.
2. Add the red pepper and anchovy fillets with capers and oil and process to a purée, about 10 seconds.
3. Add fromage frais, tomato purée, lemon juice, garlic and parsley. Season lightly with the black pepper.
4. Process until smooth (8–10 seconds).
5. Turn into a paté dish and serve with the accompaniments.

Mixed Cheese Paté

A must for cheese lovers, this paté will be particularly popular at Christmas time. Use the reduced fat cheeses that are now readily available, which give you all the flavour with about half the fat.

Serves 6

30ml (2 tablespoons) snipped chives
100g (4oz) reduced fat mature Cheddar cheese, cubed
100g (4oz) Dolcelatte blue cheese, cubed
100g (4oz) reduced fat soft cheese
15ml (1 tablespoon) mild wholegrain mustard
50g (2oz) polyunsaturated low fat spread

To serve
sprigs of fresh parsley
wholemeal crackers
celery, apples and grapes

1. Put the chives into the food processor. Using the metal blade, process until finely chopped.
2. Add the Cheddar and Dolcelatte cheeses and chop finely.
3. Add the reduced fat soft cheese with the mustard and the low fat spread. Process for about 10 seconds, until smooth and creamy.
4. Spoon the paté into a serving dish, smooth over the top, then cover and chill for at least 30 minutes.
5. Serve, garnished with the parsley and accompanied by the wholemeal crackers, celery and fruit.

Soured Cream Coleslaw with Walnuts

This pretty coleslaw uses red cabbage and celery with a light creamy dressing. The dried apricots add a subtle sweetness. Delicious with cold chicken or cheese dishes.

Serves 4

225g (8oz) red cabbage
½ medium onion, peeled and quartered
2 sticks celery, each cut into 4
2 large carrots
50g (2oz) ready to use dried apricots, chopped roughly with scissors
1 150ml (5fl oz) carton soured cream
A little sea salt and freshly ground black pepper
50g (2oz) walnuts

1. Using the slicing disc, slice the red cabbage and the onion. Turn into a large mixing bowl.
2. Using the metal blade, chop the celery finely, then change to the grating disc and grate the carrots. Add to the bowl.
3. Add the apricots with the soured cream. Season with the salt and pepper. Toss well.
4. Process the walnuts very briefly using the metal blade and sprinkle over the coleslaw to serve.

Curried Pasta Salad

Use either mayonnaise from the recipe in this book (see p. 183), or a commercially made variety. The combination of fruits with the flavour of curry is delicious and will be very popular. Serve this salad on the buffet table.

Serves 4

225g (8oz) pasta shapes, cooked according to directions on the packet, then drained and rinsed with plenty of cold water
2 fresh peaches or nectarines, stoned
1 green pepper, de-seeded and cut into 4
1 red pepper, de-seeded and cut into 4
1 large tomato, quartered
2.5ml (½ teaspoon) curry powder
60ml (4 tablespoons) mayonnaise
15ml (1 tablespoon) semi-skimmed milk
15ml (1 tablespoon) apricot jam
A little sea salt and freshly ground black pepper
30ml (2 tablespoons) freshly chopped parsley or coriander

1. Put the drained pasta into a large mixing bowl – leaving a little cold water on the pasta will help the mayonnaise dressing stick to it.
2. Put the peaches or nectarines, red and green pepper and the tomato into the food processor, using the metal blade. Process briefly, to chop roughly. Turn into the bowl with the pasta. Toss lightly.
3. Blend together the curry powder, mayonnaise, milk, apricot jam and a little seasoning. Add to the salad and mix well.
4. Serve immediately, sprinkled with the parsley or coriander.

Carrot, Celery and Chick Pea Salad

The combination of colours and textures in this salad is attractive and tasty. A nutritious salad that proves very popular whenever it's served.

Serves 6

3 medium carrots
4 sticks celery, cut into pieces
1 200g (7oz) can sweetcorn kernels with peppers, drained
1 430g (15oz) can chick peas, drained
50g (2oz) walnuts, chopped

For the dressing
60ml (4 tablespoons) bottled vinaigrette
15ml (1 tablespoon) freshly chopped parsley

1. Using the grating disc on the food processor, grate the carrot. Transfer to a large mixing bowl.
2. Using the metal blade chop the celery coarsely. Add to the mixing bowl.
3. Add the sweetcorn, chick peas and vinaigrette to the bowl with the parsley. Toss to coat.
4. Turn into an attractive salad bowl and serve immediately, sprinkled with the chopped nuts.

Broccoli and Potato Salad with Spring Onions

Crisp, blanched broccoli contrasts well with tasty new potatoes. The mayonnaise should lightly coat the ingredients without destroying their texture.

Serves 4 to 6

450g (1lb) small new potatoes, preferably Jersey Royals
2 sprigs fresh mint
225g (8oz) small broccoli florets
45ml (3 tablespoons) vinaigrette
250ml (8fl oz) thick mayonnaise (see p. 183)
4 spring onions
30ml (2 tablespoons) chives

1. Wash and scrub the new potatoes and place them in a large saucepan. Cover with boiling water and bring back to the boil. Simmer, covered, for approximately 15 minutes, until tender. Drain and turn into a mixing bowl.
2. Put broccoli in a separate saucepan. Cover with boiling water. Bring back to the boil, then cover and simmer for 2–3 minutes. Drain and add to the mixing bowl. Add vinaigrette and toss gently to coat. Set aside to cool completely.
3. Add mayonnaise and continue to toss until coated with the dressing. Turn into a serving bowl.
4. Just before serving, using the metal blade on the food processor, chop the spring onions and chives for about 7 seconds. Sprinkle over the salad.

Fruity Cabbage Salad

This crisp salad served in a coleslaw dressing with orange juice added is good with game and other poultry dishes. Try it also with barbecue dishes and sliced cold meats.

Serves 6

½ head Chinese leaves, cut to fit machine
225g (8oz) red cabbage, cut to fit machine
100g (4oz) fresh bean sprouts
1 large green pepper, de-seeded and cut into 4
2 spring onions
1 red or green eating apple
25g (1oz) raisins
25g (1oz) dried apricots, chopped

For the dressing
90ml (6 tablespoons) mayonnaise (see p. 183)
60ml (4 tablespoons) orange juice or juice made from 1 orange on the juicer
rind ½ orange, grated
A little sea salt and freshly ground black pepper

1. Using the slicing disc on the food processor, shred the Chinese leaves then transfer them to a large mixing bowl.
2. Shred the red cabbage and add to the bowl with the bean sprouts.
3. Change to the metal blade and chop the pepper with the spring onions. Add to the bowl.
4. Core and slice the apple, then chop roughly using the metal blade on the machine and add to the bowl.
5. In a small bowl, blend the mayonnaise and orange juice together. Add the orange rind and season lightly.
6. Pour the dressing over the salad and add the raisins and apricots.
7. Toss the ingredients together lightly to coat. Serve immediately.

Supper Salad

A filling mid-week salad that the family will love. Serve on a bed of lettuce with chunks of wholemeal bread.

Serves 4

225g (8oz) white cabbage
3 sticks celery
2 red apples
1 7.5cm (3in) piece cucumber, cut into 3 pieces
225g (8oz) Sopocka Polish sausage

For the dressing
45ml (3 tablespoons) olive oil
30ml (2 tablespoons) lime juice
A little sea salt and freshly ground black pepper

To serve
washed lettuce leaves

1. Using the slicing disc on the food processor, slice the cabbage and celery. Transfer to a large mixing bowl.
2. Core and slice the apples, then chop them roughly on the processor, using the metal blade. Add to the bowl.
3. Chop the cucumber roughly, using the metal blade. Add to the bowl.
4. Cut the sausage into strips and add to the bowl.
5. Prepare the dressing. Mix the olive oil and lime juice together in a mug. Season with the salt and pepper. Whisk lightly with a fork and add to the salad.
6. Gently toss the salad ingredients together to coat with the dressing.
7. Arrange a bed of lettuce on a large plate. Top with the prepared salad and serve immediately.

Tomato Soup

This quick and easy soup is made from healthy store cupboard ingredients. Try it piping hot on a winter evening accompanied by garlic bread.

Serves 4 to 6

1 onion, chopped
15ml (1 tablespoon) olive oil
350g (12oz) carrots, diced
1 400g (14oz) can chopped tomatoes with herbs
900ml (1½ pints) vegetable stock

To serve
45ml (3 tablespoons) freshly chopped parsley

1. In a large saucepan, soften the onion in the heated oil for about 5 minutes.
2. Add the carrots and sauté for a further 5 minutes.
3. Add the tomatoes with any juice, then stir in the stock. Cover and simmer for 20 minutes.
4. Using the metal blade, turn the tomato mixture into the food processor and process until smooth. (You may have to do this in two batches.)
5. Return to the pan and reheat gently to serving temperature. Serve immediately, sprinkled with the chopped parsley.

This recipe makes approximately 1.3 litres (2¼ pints) soup.

Watercress Soup

Serve this well flavoured soup either hot in the winter or chilled during the summer months. Ideal for dinner parties.

Serves 4

30ml (2 tablespoons) corn oil
1 bunch spring onions, roughly chopped
2 bunches watercress, de-stalked
2 medium potatoes
1 clove garlic, chopped
15ml (1 tablespoon) wholemeal flour
A little sea salt and freshly ground black pepper
900ml (1½ pints) light chicken or vegetable stock
150ml (5fl oz) sour cream

1. Heat the oil in a large, heavy based saucepan, then add the spring onions and sauté for about 5 minutes until they start to soften.
2. Chop the watercress in the food processor using the metal blade, then slice the potatoes using the slicing disc.
3. Add the potatoes and watercress to the pan with the garlic and continue to sauté for a further 5 minutes. Stir in the flour.
4. Season lightly, then add the stock. Bring to the boil, cover, and simmer for 20 minutes. Remove from the heat and allow to cool.
5. Process the soup in the food processor, using the metal blade, until blended; you may need to do this in two batches.
6. Return to the saucepan and stir in the soured cream. If serving cold, chill until ready to serve.
7. If serving hot, reheat to serving temperature, without boiling.

This recipe makes approximately 1.2 litres (2 pints) soup.

Speedy Mushroom Soup

This creamy soup is simple and quick to make and uses fresh ingredients for a rich flavour. Use freshly made chicken stock, or low salt stock cubes from a health food store – most cubes found in supermarkets are particularly high in salt (sodium). A little butter is used in this recipe, for flavour.

Serves 4

1 small onion, peeled and cut into 4
1 clove garlic, peeled
25g (1oz) butter
225g (8oz) button mushrooms
30ml (2 tablespoons) plain wholemeal flour
600ml (1 pint) chicken or vegetable stock
150ml (5fl oz) semi-skimmed milk

To serve
chopped chives

1. Using the metal blade, process the onion with the garlic for a few seconds, until finely chopped.
2. Melt the butter in a large saucepan, then sauté the onion and garlic for 3–4 minutes, until softened.
3. Meanwhile, process the mushrooms, using the metal blade, until finely chopped.
4. Stir the flour into the onions and cook, stirring, for 1–2 minutes; then stir in the stock with the milk and the chopped mushrooms. Bring to the boil, stirring, then simmer for 10 minutes, stirring occasionally.
5. Serve immediately, sprinkled with the chopped chives.

This recipe makes approximately 900ml (1½ pints) soup.

Vegetable Medley with Tomato Sauce

A healthy vegetarian supper dish with lots of fibre and plenty of vitamins. This recipe is quickly cooked in the microwave and tastes delicious with the cashew nut and sunflower seed topping. Serve with chunks of wholemeal bread or brown rice. To toast the cashew nuts and the sunflower seeds quickly and easily, spread them out on a dinner plate and microwave on 100 per cent/FULL power for 2 minutes. Rearrange and microwave for a further 2 minutes.

Serves 4

1 clove garlic
1 medium onion, peeled and cut into 4
4 medium carrots
2 medium courgettes
1 small cauliflower, broken into florets

For the sauce
1 400g (14oz) can chopped tomatoes
½ handful mixed fresh herbs (parsley, basil, oregano, thyme)

To serve
50g (2oz) cashew nuts (toasted)
25g (1oz) sunflower seeds (toasted)

1. Using the metal blade on the food processor, chop the garlic and onion fairly finely. Transfer to a 1.75 litre (3 pint) casserole dish that is suitable for the microwave.
2. Using the slicing disc, slice the carrots and courgettes and add to the casserole with the cauliflower florets. Add 60ml (4 tablespoons) water. Cover.
3. Microwave on 100 per cent/FULL power for about 10 minutes, stirring and re-covering once, half way through. Set aside covered whilst you prepare the sauce.
4. Using the metal blade, empty the can of tomatoes into the blender. Add the herbs. Process until puréed.
5. Transfer the tomato sauce to a saucepan and heat gently, stirring continuously.
6. Pour the sauce over the vegetables and serve immediately, topped with the toasted cashew nuts and sunflower seeds.

Smoked Haddock Crumble

Fish cooked lightly to perfection, coated with a sauce, then topped with a crispy savoury crumble – a delicious lunch or supper dish that makes a filling meal when served with a salad.

Serves 4

750g (1½lb) smoked haddock
1 leek
40g (1½oz) polyunsaturated margarine
50g (2oz) wholemeal flour
600ml (1 pint) semi-skimmed milk
2 eggs, size 3, hard boiled
A little sea salt and freshly ground black pepper

For the crumble topping
150g (5oz) plain wholemeal flour
50g (2oz) polyunsaturated margarine
50g (2oz) reduced fat Cheddar cheese

1. Arrange the fish, in a single layer, in a shallow dish. Add 30ml (2 tablespoons) water. Cover and microwave on 100 per cent/FULL power for approximately 7–9 minutes, until cooked.
2. Using the slicing disc on the food processor, slice the leek.
3. Heat the margarine in a medium size saucepan and fry the leek until softened, approximately 5 minutes.
4. Pre-heat the oven to gas mark 5, 375°F (190°C).
5. Stir in the flour and cook for a further minute.
6. Gradually add the milk. Bring to the boil, stirring, then continue to cook for 2–3 minutes, still stirring, until the sauce boils and thickens.
7. Using the metal blade, chop the egg and add to the sauce, then flake in the fish, with any juices.
8. Turn into a 1.75 litre (3 pint) oven proof dish.
9. Using the metal blade, put the flour into the processor bowl and add the margarine and cheese. Process to chop finely. Sprinkle over the fish mixture.
10. Bake for 35 minutes, until golden. Serve immediately.

Cheesy Nut and Vegetable Roast

Vegetarians will love this cheesy roast. Delicious hot or cold, served in slices with salad and a fromage frais or mayonnaise based dressing. You will need a 900g (2lb) loaf tin, lightly greased and bottom lined.

Serves 6

175g (6oz) easy cook long grain brown rice
15ml (1 tablespoon) olive oil
1 leek
2 medium carrots
1 medium parsnip
100g (4oz) button mushrooms
2 slices wholemeal bread, crusts removed
100g (4oz) fresh peanuts, husks removed
50g (2oz) Danish Blue cheese
50g (2oz) mature Cheddar cheese
2 eggs, size 2
A little sea salt and freshly ground black pepper

1. Pre-heat the oven to gas mark 4, 350°F (180°C).
2. Cook the rice in boiling water for approximately 25 minutes, according to the directions on the packet. Drain well.
3. Meanwhile, slice the well-washed leek in the food processor, using the slicing disc. Turn into a large mixing bowl.
4. Using the grating disc on the food processor, grate the carrots and the parsnip, and add to the bowl.
5. Using the metal blade, chop the mushrooms and bread finely. Add to the bowl.
6. Chop the peanuts with both types of cheese, using the metal blade. Add to the bowl.
7. Stir in the drained rice with the beaten eggs and a seasoning of salt and pepper. Mix well.
8. Pack the mixture into the loaf tin. Level the top. Cover with a piece of foil.
9. Bake for 1–1¼ hours until firm to the touch. Serve hot or cold, in slices, with a fromage frais dressing or a tomato sauce.

Potato Leek Bake

A tasty potato dish that's superfast to prepare and goes well with almost any family meal.

Serves 4

900g (2lb) potatoes, peeled and cut to fit tube
1 leek
2 cloves garlic, crushed
150ml (5fl oz) semi-skimmed milk
150ml (5fl oz) vegetable stock
15ml (1 tablespoon) freshly snipped chives
A little sea salt and freshly ground black pepper
50g (2oz) reduced fat Cheddar cheese, grated

1. Pre-heat the oven to gas mark 4, 350°F (180°C).
2. Lightly oil a 1.75 litre (3 pint) oven proof dish.
3. Using the slicing disc, slice the potatoes in the food processor, then put them into a colander and rinse well under cold running water. Dry on a clean tea towel.
4. Put the potatoes into a large pan. Slice the leeks on the machine and add them to the pan with the garlic, milk, stock and chives. Season with a little salt and pepper.
5. Bring slowly to boiling point, then simmer for 5 minutes.
6. Pour mixture into the prepared dish and sprinkle evenly with the grated cheese.
7. Bake for 40–45 minutes until golden. Serve immediately.

Stir-fried Cauliflower, Peppers and Cashew Nuts

Cauliflower sliced in the food processor turns into slim attractive shapes that cook fast and are ideal for stir-fry recipes. A crunchy vegetable dish.

Serves 4

50g (2oz) cashew nuts
1 small onion, peeled and quartered
1 red pepper, de-seeded and cut into 4
350g (12oz) cauliflower, cut to fit tube
30ml (2 tablespoons) olive oil
120ml (4fl oz) tomato and carrot juice (see page 100)
15ml (1 tablespoon) soy sauce

1. Dry-fry the cashew nuts in a wok or large frying pan until golden. Set aside.
2. Chop the onion and the red pepper, together, in the food processor using the metal blade – allow about 5 seconds in total.
3. Slice the cauliflower using the slicing disc.
4. Heat the oil in a wok or large frying pan, then add the onion with the pepper and stir-fry for 2–3 minutes.
5. Add the cauliflower and stir-fry for a further 3 minutes.
6. Add the juice with the soy sauce.
7. Heat until boiling, then simmer for 2 minutes.
8. Serve immediately, sprinkled with the cashew nuts.

Potato and Carrot Purée

This full flavoured vegetable dish is delicious served with salads, fish or poultry dishes.

Serves 4

450g (1lb) potatoes
1 medium onion
350g (12oz) carrots
1 clove garlic, crushed
300ml (½ pint) water
60ml (4 tablespoons) soured cream
15ml (1 tablespoon) freshly chopped parsley
A little sea salt and freshly ground black pepper

1. Slice the potatoes, onion and carrots, using the slicing disc.
2. Put the potatoes into a medium saucepan with the onion, carrots, and garlic. Pour over the water.
3. Bring slowly to the boil, stirring continuously. Cover with a lid and simmer for approximately 15 minutes, until the vegetables are completely tender. Set aside for 5 minutes.
4. Drain the vegetables then put them into the food processor, using the metal blade. Add the soured cream and the parsley. Season lightly.
5. Process until puréed, stopping the machine once or twice to scrape round the sides.
6. Return to the pan and reheat thoroughly over a gentle heat, stirring continuously. Serve immediately.

Special Fried Rice

Try this home-made version of a Chinese classic that is delicious and good for you. Serve the dish on its own, with salad, or as an accompaniment to other dishes.

Serves 4

350g (12oz) easy cook brown rice
3 courgettes
100g (4oz) mushrooms
3 spring onions
30ml (2 tablespoons) olive oil
2 eggs, size 2, beaten
30ml (2 tablespoons) soy sauce
5ml (1 teaspoon) clear honey
175g (6oz) peeled prawns, defrosted if frozen

To serve
30ml (2 tablespoons) freshly chopped oregano

1. Cook the rice in plenty of boiling water for 25 minutes, until tender, then drain well and set aside.
2. Slice the courgettes in the food processor with the slicing disc. Cook them in a little boiling water until just starting to soften (about 3 minutes). Drain and set aside.
3. Chop the mushrooms and onions roughly, using the metal blade on the food processor. Set aside.
4. Heat the oil in a wok or large frying pan, then add the cooked rice and stir-fry for 3–4 minutes, until heated through.
5. Add the mushrooms and onions and continue to stir-fry for 2–3 minutes.
6. Combine the eggs with the soy sauce and honey, and add to the wok. Add the courgettes and prawns.
7. Continue to stir-fry for 3–4 minutes, until the eggs have set.
8. Serve immediately, sprinkled with the oregano.

Apple and Apricot Snow

A light, fluffy dessert that's surprisingly full of fruity flavour and very satisfying. Excellent served with wafer biscuits.

Serves 4

750g (1½lb) Bramley apples, peeled, cored and quartered to fit processor
100g (4oz) ready to use dried apricots
50ml (2fl oz) water
50g (2oz) caster sugar
2 egg whites, size 2

To serve
wafer biscuits

1. Using the slicing disc, slice the Bramley apples. Turn into a large, non-stick saucepan.
2. Roughly chop the apricots using the metal blade. Add to the pan with the water and sugar.
3. Cook the apples over a gentle heat until they soften completely, about 10 minutes, and allow to cool.
4. Using the metal blade, process the apple mixture to a purée. Remove metal blade.
5. Using a clean bowl and whisk, whisk the egg whites until stiff. Fold into the cooled purée.
6. Divide between four tall sundae dishes. Chill until ready to serve.

Redcurrant and Loganberry Mousse

A perfect pud for the midsummer months. This creamy mousse is light and refreshing. Serve it with a bowl of soft fruits: redcurrants, blackcurrants, strawberries and loganberries.

Serves 8

150g (5oz) caster sugar
100g (4oz) loganberries, hulled
225g (8oz) redcurrants, removed from stems
1 11g (0.4oz) sachet gelatine
4 eggs, size 2, separated
zest of ½ lemon
150ml (5fl oz) whipping cream, whipped to soft peak stage
85ml (3fl oz) fromage frais

To serve
assorted soft fruits

1. In a large mixing bowl, sprinkle 15ml (1 tablespoon) sugar over the loganberries and redcurrants. Set aside for 10 minutes.
2. In a small bowl, sprinkle the gelatine over 60ml (4 tablespoons) water. Set aside for 10 minutes then dissolve the gelatine over a pan of hot water, stirring continuously. Set aside.
3. Purée the loganberries and sugar in the food processor, using the metal blade.
4. In a clean bowl, beat the egg yolks with the remaining caster sugar, using the whisk attachment on the food processor, until thick and creamy, or whisk in a separate bowl with an electric whisk.
5. Fold lemon zest into the whipped mixture. Gently add the dissolved gelatine then fold in the whipping cream and the fromage frais.
6. Fold the loganberry and redcurrant purée into the creamy mixture.
7. Transfer to a large mixing bowl.
8. In a clean bowl, whisk the egg whites until stiff, using an electric mixer. Fold them in evenly and quickly.

9. Turn into an attractive glass dish and refrigerate to set.
10. Serve with soft fruits.

Blackcurrant Cheese Cake

This tangy cheese cake uses cottage cheese combined with medium fat soft cheese, to produce a healthy cheese cake all the family will love. Serve with a little single cream or one of the reduced fat ice creams now available in most supermarkets. You will need a 20cm (8in) loose-bottomed tin or spring form tin.

Serves 6 to 8

100g (4oz) digestive biscuits
25g (1oz) polyunsaturated margarine
1 11g (0.4oz) sachet gelatine
225g (8oz) cottage cheese
200g (7oz) medium fat soft cheese
1 450g (1lb) jar blackcurrants in syrup
50g (2oz) caster sugar
2 eggs, size 3, separated
10ml (2 teaspoons) arrowroot

1. Using the metal blade, break the biscuits into rough pieces and process in the food processor until crumbed.
2. Melt the margarine in a medium sized saucepan. Stir the biscuits into the margarine then press into the base of a 20cm (8in) tin. Refrigerate.
3. Sprinkle gelatine over 60ml (4 tablespoons) cold water in a small bowl. Set aside for about 5 minutes until 'spongy'.
4. Using the metal blade, process the cottage cheese for 10 seconds, until smooth. Add the soft cheese and process again, just to blend.
5. Drain the blackcurrants, reserving the juice, and add them to the food processor with the sugar, egg yolks and dissolved gelatine. Process to mix (about 10 seconds).
6. Whisk the egg whites in a clean bowl until standing in soft peaks. Fold into the cheese cake mixture evenly. Spoon on to the biscuit base and chill until set (about 2½ hours).
7. When ready to serve, blend the reserved juice with the arrowroot. Heat, stirring continuously, in a medium saucepan, until boiling and slightly thickened. Allow to cool.

8. Arrange cheese cake on a pretty serving plate. Serve with the blackcurrant sauce.

Creamy Peach and Ginger Layer

A simple quick dessert with different textures that complements any main course. Flaked almonds may now be bought, ready toasted, from most supermarkets.

Serves 4

225g (8oz) ginger biscuits
50g (2oz) flaked toasted almonds
1 400g (14oz) can peach slices in natural juice, drained
200ml (8fl oz) fromage frais
15–30ml (1–2 tablespoons) clear honey

To serve
individual glass dishes or wine glasses

1. Break the biscuits into rough pieces, and process using the metal blade, until finely chopped. Combine with the almonds and set aside.
2. Reserve four peach slices, then process the remainder with the fromage frais and honey, until smooth.
3. Put a third of the biscuit and almond mixture into the bottom of four individual glass dishes. Top with a third of the fruit mixture.
4. Continue layering in this way, until all the ingredients have been used, ending with a layer of the biscuit mixture.
5. Decorate each dish with a peach slice and serve immediately.

Apricot and Raisin Loaf Cake

This moist, fruity cake freezes well and may be stored, wrapped in the freezer, for up to three months. Excellent in the children's lunch boxes or served, sliced, with a cup of tea. Use the food processor to chop the apricots before you make the cake. You will need a 900g (2lb) loaf tin, lightly greased and base lined.

Makes 1 900g (2lb) cake

For the cake
175g (6oz) polyunsaturated margarine, at room temperature
175g (6oz) caster sugar
3 eggs, size 2
50g (2oz) raisins
100g (4oz) dried apricots, roughly chopped
225g (8oz) self-raising wholemeal flour
5ml (1 teaspoon) mixed spice

For the glaze
45ml (3 tablespoons) clear honey
15ml (1 tablespoon) lemon juice

1. Pre-heat the oven to gas mark 4, 350°F (180°C).
2. Put all the ingredients for the cake into the food processor. Using the metal blade, process for approximately 24 seconds, until blended.
3. Place in the prepared tin. Level the surface.
4. Bake just below the centre of the oven for approximately 1–1¼ hours, or until a skewer inserted in the centre comes out clean. Cover the cake with a piece of foil or greaseproof paper if it becomes too brown before it's cooked in the centre.
5. Turn out on to a wire cooling tray and allow to cool for 10 minutes.
6. In a small pan heat together the honey with the lemon juice. Brush all over the cake to glaze.
7. Allow cake to cool completely before serving.

Cinnamon Apple Cake

Tart apples baked in a cinnamon flavoured cake make a simply delicious combination. Serve small slices with fromage frais or natural yoghurt for a tea time treat. You will need a 20cm (8in) cake tin, lightly greased and bottom lined.

Makes 1 20cm (8in) fairly shallow cake

175g (6oz) polyunsaturated margarine, at room temperature
175g (6oz) soft brown sugar
3 eggs, size 3
5ml (1 teaspoon) ground cinnamon
350g (12oz) self-raising wholemeal flour
45ml (3 tablespoons) semi-skimmed milk
275g (10oz) Bramley apples, peeled and roughly chopped

1. Pre-heat the oven to gas mark 4, 350°F (180°C).
2. Using the metal blade, put the margarine, sugar, eggs, cinnamon, flour and milk into the food processor.
3. Process for approximately 25 seconds until light and fluffy, stopping the machine and scraping the mixture from the sides once or twice.
4. Add the apples and process for a few seconds, just to combine.
5. Turn the mixture into the prepared tin.
6. Bake in the middle of the oven for 1–1¼ hours, until a skewer inserted into the centre comes out clean.
7. Cool on a wire rack and serve in small squares.

Almond Biscuits

These crisp biscuits are made without fat, although there is, of course, fat in the almonds. The crushed cereal gives a good texture. Excellent in the biscuit jar instead of commercially made examples that often have a high fat and salt content. You will need two baking trays for the biscuits.

Makes 16 biscuits

50g (2oz) Weetabix
2 egg whites, size 3
5ml (1 teaspoon) almond essence
150g (5oz) caster sugar
75g (3oz) ground almonds
16 blanched almonds

1. Pre-heat the oven to gas mark 5, 375°F (190°C).
2. Put the Weetabix, broken into rough pieces, into the food processor, using the metal blade. Process to crush finely then set aside.
3. Whisk the egg whites, using the whisk attachment, until very stiff.
4. Add the almond essence, sugar, ground almonds and crushed Weetabix all in one go and turn the machine on again to mix ingredients together.
5. Prepare two baking sheets with baking parchment.
6. Take 5ml (1 teaspoon) of the mixture and roll into a ball. Place on the baking sheet and flatten slightly.
7. Repeat until all the mixture has been used up. Put an almond in the centre of each biscuit.
8. Bake in the centre of the oven until lightly golden, 10–12 minutes.
9. Allow to cool on the tins.

Healthy Honey Snack Mix

To stop kids reaching for the crisps and peanuts, keep a stock of this crunchy mixture in a glass storage jar. Ideal with milk as a cereal, too. You will need a large roasting tin for this recipe.

Makes approximately 550g (1¼lb)

4 slices wholemeal bread, from a large loaf, crusts removed
60ml (4 tablespoons) clear honey
85ml (3fl oz) corn oil
2.5ml (½ teaspoon) ground cinnamon
350g (12oz) rolled oats
50g (2oz) walnuts, roughly chopped
50g (2oz) prunes, pitted and roughly chopped
100g (4oz) dried apricots, roughly chopped
40g (1½oz) shredded coconut
50g (2oz) chopped dates

1. Pre-heat the oven to gas mark 5, 375°F (190°C).
2. Using the metal blade, tear each slice of bread into 4 and put in the processor. Process into crumbs. Set aside.
3. Put honey, oil and cinnamon into a large saucepan and heat, stirring, until completely liquid.
4. Remove the pan from the heat, then stir in the bread-crumbs and the oats. Stir really well so that the dry ingredients become coated with the honey and oil.
5. Turn the mixture into the roasting tin and spread out evenly.
6. Bake for approximately 30 minutes, stirring twice, until crisp and golden. Stir again.
7. Set aside until completely cold.
8. Stir in walnuts, prunes, apricots, coconut and dates.
9. Store in an airtight container.

Mango Milk Shake

Use the best vanilla ice cream available for this delicious recipe – that means one made with real dairy cream. We all need to spoil ourselves just once in a while and, as the recipe serves two, each person is consuming only 25g (1oz) ice cream.

Serves 2

1 mango, peeled
350ml (12fl oz) semi-skimmed milk, chilled
50g (2oz) vanilla dairy ice cream

To serve
tall tumblers

1. Slice the mango flesh, discarding the central stone, and put it into the food processor, using the metal blade.
2. Add the milk and ice cream and process for about 12 seconds.
3. Serve immediately in tall tumblers.

This recipe makes approximately 475ml (16fl oz) shake.

Peach and Strawberry Yoghurt Shake

A delicious fruity shake that's wonderful served with crushed ice. Vary the ingredients according to the fruits in season.

Serves 2

1 large peach or nectarine
6 large strawberries, halved
15ml (1 tablespoon) clear honey
150ml (5fl oz) Greek yoghurt
300ml (½ pint) semi-skimmed milk, chilled

To serve
crushed ice
tall tumblers

1. Roughly chop the peach or nectarine, discarding the central stone. Put into the food processor, using the metal blade. Add all remaining ingredients.
2. Process until smooth (about 12 seconds).
3. Put a little crushed ice into two tumblers, top up with the shake, and serve immediately.

This recipe makes approximately 550ml (18fl oz) shake.

More Cookery Non-Fiction from Headline:

GOOD HOUSEKEEPING

EATING FOR A HEALTHY Skin

ALIX KIRSTA

GOOD HOUSEKEEPING
— the recipe for healthy living

Do sweets really cause spots?
Is eczema food-related?
Does vitamin E prevent ageing?

Working on the principle that we are what we eat,
GOOD HOUSEKEEPING EATING FOR A HEALTHY
SKIN answers all these questions and more while
showing how healthy eating can make a real
difference to the way we look.

With a wide range of delicious recipes high in the
nutrients essential for a good-looking skin, GOOD
HOUSEKEEPING EATING FOR A HEALTHY SKIN
covers everything from Breakfast and Brunch to
Seasonal Salads, Puddings and Desserts.
But this is more than just a recipe book. It also
provides invaluable information on all aspects of skin
care, from preventing spots to avoiding allergies, and
gives sound advice on how best to withstand such perils
of everyday life as stress and exposure to sun
and pollution. Eat for a healthy skin and eat
for a healthy life.

Other GOOD HOUSEKEEPING titles from Headline:
Good Food for Diabetics by Theodora Fitzgibbon
Eating for a Healthy Heart by The Coronary Prevention Group

COOKERY/HEALTH   0 7472 3281 4

A selection of bestsellers from Headline